Regina's Tale
flight from Siberia

Cynthia Clark

Copyright © 2013 Cynthia Clark

All rights reserved.

ISBN:1484948327
ISBN-13: 9781484948323

DEDICATION

This is dedicated to the Polish men, women, and children who were interred during WW II in the slave labor camps of Russia, and to those who may still be there.

Cynthia Clark

KONSULAT GENERALNY
RZECZYPOSPOLITEJ POLSKIEJ
W LOS ANGELES

CONSULATE GENERAL
OF THE REPUBLIC OF POLAND
IN LOS ANGELES

Los Angeles, September 25, 2008.

Mrs. Regina Niemczycki
9361 E 1 Mile Rd
Luther, MI 49656-9391

Dear Sir,

On behalf of the President of the Republic of Poland, I am honored to bestow you with a Cross of the Exiles to Siberia. Representing the post-war generation myself, I wish to express my gratitude for your commitment and endurance in the most difficult moments in the history of our nation.

The tragedy, which you and your closest ones experienced when deported to the East by the occupant Soviet authorities, must have left a permanent mark in the history of your family. This is also reflected in the fate of hundreds of thousands of Polish citizens. Nevertheless, the unbreakable spirit and lasting faith in Polish freedom has been unifying our nation regardless of the place and living conditions.

This medal not only testifies your expatriation, but above all it highlights your character's strength, courage, and often heroic approach to the most difficult challenges that life can bring. Despite this very order being bestowed to many Polish exiles to Siberia, each of them carries a personal, unique story of the victory of good over evil.

Once again, please accept my most genuine congratulations and best wishes of health and happiness in your personal life.

Sincerely,

Paulina Kapuścińska
Consul General

12400 Wilshire Blvd., Suite 555, Los Angeles, CA 90025, Phone: (310) 442-8500, Fax: (310) 442-8515
Email: consulpila@consulpila.org, www.losangeleskg.polamb.net

Cynthia Clark

CONTENTS

Acknowledgments

Prologue

1	Regina's Tale	Pg# 1
2	Stefan Siminski	Pg # 8
3	Rejmontowicze	Pg # 16
4	February 10, 1940	Pg # 22
5	Kotlas, Siberia 1940	Pg # 28
6	Polish government-in-exile	Pg # 40
7	Amnesty	Pg # 43
8	Samarkand, Uzbekistan	Pg # 47
9	Kolkhoz	Pg # 52
10	Stalin Rescinds Amnesty	Pg # 58
11	Pahlavi, Iran	Pg# 63
12	Tehran, Iran	Pg # 68
13	Panchgani, India	Pg # 72
14	Stefan	Pg # 80
15	Anders Army	Pg # 88

16	Yalta Conference	Pg # 91
17	Journey to England	Pg # 94
18	Reunion	Pg # 98
19	Zdzislaw Niemczycki	Pg # 102
20	Release from Siberia	Pg # 107
21	Warsaw Uprising	Pg # 109
22	Wars End	Pg # 112
23	Immigration to USA	Pg # 115
	Epilogue	
	References	

ACKNOWLEDGMENTS

A very special thank you to Regina Siminski Niemczycki for sharing her story with us. To Theresa for her technical expertise and her support. Kathy Box, a friend and writer who read my draft, made suggestions and encouraged me to complete the project. To Zofia Klaczak Rombach of Grayling, Michigan, who translated the letters to Stefan.

To the members of my writing group who always give the impetus to write and rewrite.

To Chet, my husband who always has my back and continues to love me no matter what!

And finally to all of you who take the time to read this real life story of love and sacrifice. A father's struggle to keep his family together during times of desperation as told through his daughter's eyes.

PROLOGUE

I first met Regina at coffee hour in the church basement in Luther, Michigan. After mass that Sunday at St. Ignatius we were all invited down for coffee and doughnuts.

There was an article pinned on the bulletin board about a parishioner who as a young girl had been taken by the Russians and sent to Siberia. When I finished reading I turned and realized I was looking at that young girl, now a mature woman, having coffee with her friends.

The article was from our local newspaper and I wondered if Regina had ever written her life story. When I asked her, she looked up with that warm smile and a real twinkle in her eyes and said, 'Everyone asks me that but I don't know how and no one helps me.'

So began a year's journey, as a beginning writer I offered to take on the task. We learned along the way, sharing during interviews, revising, editing and finally developing her story.

There was so much about Polish history and their fight for independence that I did not know. This is also a story about her father, Stefan, who managed to keep his family together during the worst of times.

Regina is a remarkable, resilient lady with a memorable story.

Cynthia Clark

Regina's Tale - flight from Siberia

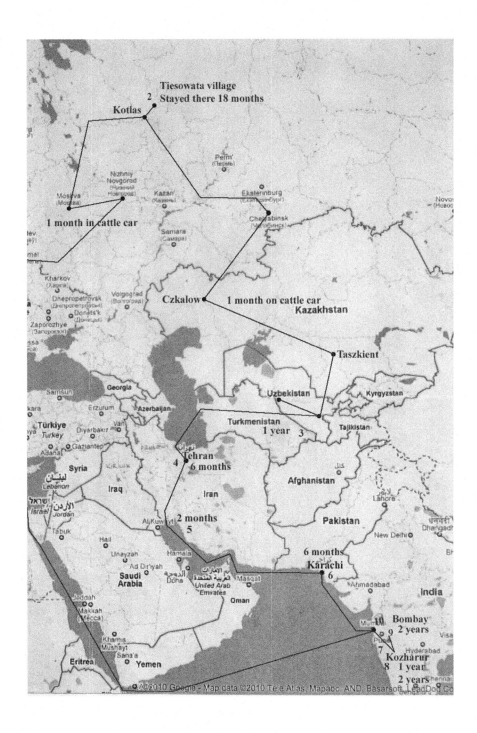

Cynthia Clark

1 REGINA'S TALE

They woke us up at two o'clock in the morning with a knock at the door. 'Otkroite!' (open up!) When my father opened the door, Russian soldiers were under every door and window. Some of them get inside the house. My father was in his night clothes. They told him to kneel in the corner, face the corner against the wall. One soldier was holding a gun to his head so he couldn't move.

'Where is your gun, where did you put your gun?!' the soldier was yelling at my father.

The war had started in September of 1939, Germans invaded Poland from the West, Russians came from the East. I didn't see Germans at all. My father was such a politician he listened to the radio to the news. He knew what would happen.

In 1940, my father knew we would be deported, that was standard procedure. The Germans had started at the Western border of Poland, divided and signed a contract how far they would go. The Russians came in on the East.

Our village was settled by veterans from World War I, the whole village, everybody, all those veterans was taken away. They suspected my father had a gun, they were after him, where was the gun?!

All during 1939 and 1940 my parents had to watch because the Ukrainians would make forays into our village. They would rob us. I think my father had buried the gun. We had a library, a lot of books and he had put them in boxes and buried them.

Then the Russian soldier said, 'Pack your things, you have fifteen minutes!'

I remember my mother took the bedspread and all the bedding tied it in a bundle. Whatever was in the wardrobe she just wrapped it and tied it in a bundle, the night before she washed it, everything was wet, she took it. I was in pajamas, in night gown, I started crying, so scared. Five of us kids, mother and father, we were all there. Edmund, my oldest brother was seventeen, Irene was thirteen, Cecylia who was fifteen was at school so she wasn't there. She was never with us. Zenon was six and Jan only four. They took everybody in the village, there was nobody left.

There were two sleds, one was for sitting and the other one packed with belongings. They let my father bring his tools, he was a lumberjack. He wrapped his tools into a bundle. The soldiers took it and put his name on it and put it on a sleigh. My parents knew we were going forever so they took pots and pans, they knew we couldn't buy them. We left everything, they took us to school and from school got us to railroad station, twenty miles or more by sleds.

Poland has always been a corridor between Germany on the West and Russia in the East, and in 1939 it was once more torn apart. When Hitler's war machines ate up the Polish landscape and his tanks invaded the country there were 1,000,000 men in the Polish Armed Forces. Ill equipped to face the military might of Germany they were soon defeated, and in September of that year Hitler and Stalin dismembered Poland. Josef Stalin, ruler of Russia, and Adolph Hitler, dictator of Germany divided the country like a loaf of bread.

The Western section went to Germany, and Russia claimed the East. Stalin had tens of thousands of Poles carted off to slave labor camps in Siberia or to the infamous Lubyanka prison, while Hitler had captured Polish soldiers sent to his prisoner of war camps.

The following year, on the tenth of February in 1940 the Soviets began a systematic deportation of the local Polish people from Eastern Poland. These specially transferred settlers, called 'spetspieresedlentsy', were deported under a secret administrative ruling.

The NKVD (**N**ardonyy **K**omissariat **V**nutrernikh **D**el) was put in charge. They were the Russian secret police who ran the Gulag system of forced labor. Besides mass deportations, they were responsible for suppressing underground resistance and executions. Like their German counterpart, the SS (**S**chut**z**staffel) they were specially trained, fierce and brutal.

To take the citizens unaware, instructions were given to begin the roundups early in the morning hours. Soldiers from Russia's Red Army, dressed in heavy winter coats, their boots covered with snow, arrived on the outskirts of the village in the dark of the night. 'You will proceed as directed, all of you at the same time will surround the houses.' More directions followed as each commander addressed his troops.

Each group was accompanied by a Polish official who sympathized with the Russians. He would read from a prepared list the names of the occupants living in each house.

'Otkroite!' ('Open up!') Soldiers with rifles that had fixed bayonets on the end pushed through the open door. The names were read. Missing persons were noted to be dealt with later. The families were then given fifteen minutes to pack their belongings and get out. This included the elderly or sick, even the dying, everyone was to be taken.

They were given no reason for the arrest. Deportations proceeded along well-tested previously prepared guidelines which had changed little from the days of the

Tsars. Generations of Poles had been dumped in the tundra or the steppes of Russia in 1832, 1864, 1906 and now in 1940.

First, families of political leaders, policemen, and border guards were taken. Next, former army personnel and government workers, finally, white collar workers, even those people the Soviets just didn't like, and those who had fled the German armies that were invading Poland from the West were forced from their homes.

Under the heading, 'Strictly Secret Instructions' were seven pages of directives that were to be followed for the removal of anti-Soviet elements from the Baltic Republics.

They included the number of armed personnel to be used in each village and city, the day and time of the action, and the means of transportation to be used. Wagons, sleighs and tumbrels (little carts used to haul animal waste) were to be confiscated from the neighboring farms to carry prisoners to the railroad stations.

The instructions were explicit allowing certain household items and excluding others. Small agricultural stocks – axes, saws - were to be tied together and packed separately, loaded into special wagons. The families were told to bring along a month's supply of food.

Then the deportees were to be loaded into railway cars by families. An estimate of twenty-five persons to a car was to be observed. After the railway car had been filled it would be locked.

It was all laid out in plans that had been used in the First World War and in the time of the Tsars.

The winter of 1940, in subzero weather, the deportations were carried out but specific instructions weren't always followed. Families became separated, belongings were confiscated and the boxcars severely overcrowded. The one order that was followed was that each car was locked securely after it was filled.

Regina Siminski was ten years old when the banging on the door woke her from a deep winter's sleep. Dressed in her night gown, she went to the doorway that separated the two room house. She stared in horror at the soldier holding a gun to her father's head.

He had on a winter great coat and hat, the ear flaps were up. On the front of the hat was an embossed red star.

Light from the lantern and the dying embers of the stove threw the room into shadows. Through her tears she saw other soldiers who stood around the room with their rifles in front of them, bayonets fixed. The light reflected off the steel blades; it would be years of nightmares before the sight would dim but never completely leave her memory.

Stefan and Ann Siminski had prepared for this day. They had heard tales which had been handed down over generations, of transports and exile, about the knock on the door and the long treks to Siberia. Stefan knew how to act, not as a fighter but to look to his family's needs and for opportunities. He took charge, told Ann what to pack, instructed the children to dress in warm clothes. Ann followed his orders, dumping everything they needed on the bed sheet. Clothing, kitchen utensils, leaving behind pillows and nonessentials. There was no room for pictures.

As they left the house Stefan grabbed the bag of millet he kept by the door.

The Siminski family was forced from their home. Like all the other villagers they were loaded up on a cart, sled or truck, whatever transportation was available. Soldiers surrounded each vehicle; they kept their rifles in front of them. No one would be allowed to escape.

Regina and her family were leaving behind household belongings, livestock and their farm. The supply of new wood was left piled by the side of their house. The extra room Stefan planned to build was left for someone else.

They would never see Rejmontowicze, their village again.

2 STEFAN SIMINSKI

My father had a really, really rich life. He was born 21st of March in 1897 in village of Zaspy, Poland. But when he was fifteen he escaped from home and went to Hamburg, Germany. There was a ship was loading and a really rich American with lots of suitcases. My father grabbed one or two of the cases and went on the boat, he never came out, he was a stow away.

My father never went to school because it was occupied by Germans. They taught German in school, German only, my grandparents said, 'You're not going to school, Germans aren't going to teach you.' He went instead to the organist from his church to get lessons. He could speak five languages, he was self taught. My father could tell you all the Popes from St. Peter, he could tell you all the English Kings, everything.

He went to Detroit, he was there for five years from 1913. Because he knew someone from the village who was there.

In 1917 he joined the army, but not the American army. He joined the volunteer Polish army that was organizing in Canada.

He fought in France, all the way to Poland. In 1920 communist Russia already had hit Poland, there was a big fight (war) by Warsaw. Russia had a huge army, hundreds of thousand Russians. My father joined the Polish army and they beat the Russians, if they hadn't Europe would be communist. They stopped communist from spreading.

The country that gave us Copernicus, who discovered the solar system, Marie Curie, who gave us radium and polonium, and musicians Chopin, Paderewski, and Arthur Rubinstein ceased to exist between the years 1772 and 1918.

Poland was completely wiped off the world map. Their land was divided and controlled by Prussians on the West and Russia on the East.

Until World War I in 1917 the country of Poland would be known as Germany/Austrian Hungarian/Prussia. The Polish language was suppressed by both the Russians and the Germans. Children were forced to learn the invaders' brand of education.

But they could not suppress the indomitable Polish spirit. Families spoke the Polish language in private and passed on their traditions and proverbs. Catholicism continued to be the predominant religion.

Into this political and oppressed time Stefan Siminski was born in the village of Zaspy. For the next fifteen years he lived with his family in the Western part of the German/Austrian Empire.

Between 1860 and 1917, 2.5 million people left Poland in search of a better and freer economic life. Almost all of them came from the rural class - so called 'Zachleben' (for bread) immigrants. These new arrivals to the United States tended to cluster in industrial cities in the Midwest. In Pennsylvania they became miners, Chicago - meat packers, Pittsburgh - steel workers, and in Detroit, eventually they would become auto workers.

Letters from relatives and other villagers who had already made the trip arrived back in Poland. They described a life of freedom, freedom to worship, to speak, to work as you wished. They encouraged others to join them.

Stories of previous stowaways and their adventures also made the rounds. Men and young boys, even women dressed as men, became stowaways. It wasn't unusual for one of them to use a visitor's pass to get on a ship then fail to disembark. Some walked on and hid in the baggage area or the ballast container. One adventurous young man strolled among the deck passengers, joining them for meals. Sleeping wherever he could hoping not to be caught.

But many were caught, often by deck hands, others when they tried to go ashore. The unsuccessful were returned to their villages only to try again.

Hamburg, the major transportation hub in Northern Germany, was the birth for the many shipping lines that transported Polish immigrants to America. Among them was the 'Hamburg American Shipping' line which sailed directly from Hamburg to Philadelphia.

The 'Hansa' Line also offered passage to the United States but by going through Canada. It even provided land transport through the Canadian Pacific railroad.

To cross the Atlantic meant two weeks at sea in conditions that were fairly harsh. On the ship Prince Oskar, the accommodations chosen by many of the immigrants was 'Zwischendeck', steerage or 'tween' decks.

It was crowded accommodations, with stale air and unwashed bodies. Meals were supplemented by whatever the immigrants brought with them.

Stefan traveled like many of the stowaways, full of grit and shaky confidence, he grabbed some suitcases and boarded a ship bound for the United States. Of all the entry ports into America, Ellis Island in New York was the most rigorous. Anyone could be detained and deported for an illness, the lack of proper papers or for not having a patron or sponsor.

The port city of Philadelphia and Boston were far more lenient, but transport through Canada was the easiest. Canada didn't bother about detaining anybody because of illness or improper papers. They seemed all too anxious to have the immigrants migrate to the United States.

Stefan made the passage safely and ended up in Detroit, Michigan where he lived for the next five years.

Detroit had two large Polish communities, one was concentrated in Poletown and the other in the city of Hamtramck. When the Dodge brothers opened an automobile plant in 1914 it provided many members of the immigrant Polish community with employment.

The Poles thrived and made a new life for themselves establishing their own societies, among them the Polish National Alliance, the Polish Roman Catholic Union and the Polish American Congress. Established families sponsored and sent for relatives and friends from the 'old' country. They celebrated both paczki day and Pulaski Day with parades and parties, dressed in traditional blouses and petticoats covered by bright colored embossed shirts.

Stefan soon found work and social contacts through friends and these local clubs.

Then on June 28, 1914, the Austrian Archduke Franz Ferdinand was assassinated in Sarajevo. This would be the shot heard around the world which started World War I.

On August 19 Germany invaded Belgium and marched toward Paris, France. In the East they crushed Russia; it wasn't until three years later in 1917 that America declared war on Germany.

Already established in the Detroit Polish community Stefan sat around talking politics with the other men. They were well aware of the current world conditions and at the age of twenty in 1917 Stefan joined the army, but not the American army.

On September 28, 1917 a Polish Army camp had been established in Niagara-on-the-Lake in Ontario, Canada. It accepted Polish volunteers who came from the United States. The camp remained active for the next eighteen months. During that time thousands of fully trained Polish Army soldiers were transported from there to Europe. The recruits wore gray blue French issue uniforms and came to be known as the 'Blue Army.' They excelled on the battle fields of France and later in the Soviet-Polish War of 1919/1920.

Stefan, as a soldier in this army, returned to his homeland through France where he fought against Germany.

In 1919 the Treaty of Versailles that ended World War I also acknowledged Poland as an independent state. Still it's borders were unsettled and within months the Poles began to clash with their neighbors. Jozef Pilsudski, Poland's Chief of State, saw an opportunity to reclaim some of the land lost in the eighteenth century. He thought it would create a buffer against future German and Soviet expansion.

Poland occupied Kiev in the Ukraine in May 1920 and skirmishes with the Russians erupted into open warfare. The Polish-Soviet war began in 1920 and saw the Poles pushed back to Warsaw. They rallied, and eventually their forces drove the Soviets out of Poland.

When the war began, Stefan rejoined the Polish Army and fought in the Battle of Warsaw against the Russians.

Joseph Stalin, a young man at the time, also joined the army (the Russian army) and fought in the same battle. He would never forget nor forgive the Polish people for the defeat. When he became head of the Soviet government, he would have his revenge by having the Polish veterans and their families shot or deported to Soviet labor camps during World War II.

The Peace of Riga, signed on March 18, 1921, ended the war and divided the disputed territories between Poland and Soviet Russia. This treaty would hold until September of 1930.

Medals were rarely awarded by the Polish army, initially individual awards of distinction were discouraged. It was considered undemocratic to single out an individual.

Poland's highest decoration, the Order of Virtuti Militari, was awarded for gallantry in the field. Only 26,000 persons from 1792 to the end of WW I were awarded this medal.

The Order of the White Eagle was given to only 1,258, the Cross of Valor to 30,000 and the Cross of Merit to 60,000.

Considering all of the Polish Officers and enlisted men from 1705 to 1945 (a period of 240 years) this is a very small number of medals.

Because of his efforts in the Polish-Soviet war, Stefan was part of the select few to receive a medal, quite likely the Fifth Class Virtuti Militari medal. Along with this he received a pension and a homestead.

The land once owned by a Polish aristocratic family had been allocated by the government to be subdivided into farm plots and given to decorated veterans of the War.

Stefan was given a section of this land and he relocated to the village of Rejmontowicze along with other veterans. He became a small farmer while continuing his trade as an accomplished lumberjack in the surrounding forests.

In 1939 hearing the news of approaching war, WW II, he and many others buried their medals and possessions near their homes. They hoped to retrieve them when peace was restored.

Stefan Siminski

3 REJMONTOWICZE

After the war, my father, he got a homestead on Eastern part of Poland in the village of Rejmontowicze.

Rejmontowicze had been mostly used by aristocrats before the war, afterwards it was divided and given as homesteads for those who were in the service. So only young families lived there.

My father got ten Hectares of land, one hectare of forest, one of grass and the rest fields. Everyone had ten Hectares, the village was divided like a T.

He had animals, chickens, pigs, everything else, it was a small farm. It was very fertile ground, my father worked the land and the forest, he was a lumberjack. He knew everything about trees.

There was a school but because there were only young people in the village we only went up to the fourth grade. Our village church was in Beresteczko, about five kilometers away.

When my father was twenty five he married my mother Ann, she would have been twenty. That was in 1923. They had six children. Edmund was born in 1923, Cecylia in 1925, Irene in 1927, I was born in 1930 and Zenon in 1934. The youngest, Jan, was born in 1936.

Ann   Edmund   Stefan   Cecylia

Irene   Aunt Stanislawa   Regina (age three)

There was another baby born in the camp in Russia but she died and I never saw her.

We had a primitive house, two rooms, my father was going to start building to add on to the house and he was buying lumber in 1930. I know they were bringing lumber to build better house but the lumber stayed behind.

There were eight of us in just two rooms. Because the farms were ten Hectares each we were very close to our neighbors. We didn't have village parties but the grownups used to have some, like a New Years Eve party.

My mother was a very good cook, lots of people would come to our house. We had cherries galore, not like here the tart and bing kind. We had about one hundred different trees, everyone had different cherries, they had bitter, sweet, cherry, summer. My mother used to make perogi with cherries.

Once a year they killed a pig, you didn't run to the store, we had kielbasa only on holidays. My mother made her own bread, we had our own garden so we would have fruit, salad, sauerkraut, everything.

We didn't have store bought toys, they were too expensive, once in a while we got a piece of candy, a hard ball or maybe a crescent roll. We used to make by ourselves dolls out of piece of rags. For the boys my father would cut a wheel and make a hoop.

The village church was Catholic, matter of fact I don't have no birth certificate or nothing, because when you were baptized all the papers was in the church. When it was bombed all the papers were burned. I made my First

Communion in 1939, that was the only time I was to confession and communion. For the two years I was in Russia, no churches or anything because Russia is atheist. I finished second grade, in 1939 they closed the school and arrested the teacher.

I remember when we were already in Iran I was in hospital, an old priest, I can still see him. I had pellagra and dysentery, he came and was going to give me communion. I said I don't know how to confess because I forgot after two years. We prayed but there was no church.

My father was such a politician he listened to the radio to the news. For twenty years it was a period of peace. Then in 1939 and 1940 the Ukrainians would make forays into our village. They would rob us, all the time my parents had to watch out. I never saw any Germans.

The whole village, everybody, all of those were veterans so when the Russians came all of them were taken away. They suspected that my father had a gun, I think he buried it. We had a library with many books, my parents put them into boxes and buried them when the Ukrainians started coming into the village.

My father knew what was coming, he was member of Polish guards, was secret society or something, very political. He kept a bag of millet by the door.

4 FEBRUARY 10, 1940

Two O'clock in the morning they took us. It was forty degrees below zero. They took everybody in the village, there was nobody left. The Ukrainians took over the village, because there were cows, horses all our belongings. The soldiers said you had fifteen minutes to pack. There were five of us kids, mother and father, older brother Edmund (seventeen), older sister Irene was next, Cecylia was at school not at home so she never was with us. I saw her after twenty three years when she came to the States in 1962.

We went by sleigh to the railway. They put forty people to one boxcar, there were no seats. Two boards were on the sides of the car, there was one side than another side, a small pot belly stove in the middle for heating and cooking. Your luggage was on the lower deck (board), upper deck for sleeping, people sleeping like sardines.

There was a hole in the floor, they put a blanket around it, it went straight down under the train. There was bars in the window, small windows only, then they locked the door.

Every two or three days the Russian soldiers, I can still see them, they release two or three box cars at a time. They would stand shoulder to shoulder with guns with bayonets on; with hats with spikes on the top. It was February, forty degrees below zero. They let you out to stretch your legs in an area of a small room.

Every train car had two people with a bucket, they would be let go to get water. That was all the water you had, they don't wash or nothing, it was just drinking and cooking. For twenty years I was afraid, I dreamt soldiers were chasing me.

My mother had taken some bedding, she was bundling it and tying it into a bedspread. We had only what we took. They had a bag of millet, we had very little food, everybody was to themselves - no sharing. Everyone used the potbelly stove to cook on.

Because we were on an irregular train we had to stop if another train was coming, they put us to one side so they could pass.

We had young strong men from our village. One was single and he said when the soldiers came every night to count us, they came and counted us to see if everybody was there. And, Waba, he said he knew Russian and he said to the soldiers, 'If you don't bring me a bottle of Vodka I'm going to escape.'

There was small windows with bars on it and just before we hit Russian border my father helped him. He was on the top deck, they somehow removed those bars. At night he sneaked out, we were in a valley, the banks were higher and my father watched. He got out the window and dropped, he get up so he didn't hurt himself, it was still the old Polish border, he get away. The next day the Russians came with a bottle of Vodka, 'Where is Waba?' 'He escaped,' my father tell them. They didn't do nothing, just laughed. Waba was just a drunk and they knew it.

For a whole month we did this, we were always frightened.

We arrived in Kotlas, Siberia in March 5th.

The trains were long green Russian box cars which snaked out of sight, the head and tail hidden around the bends in the tracks. They were high off the ground; most of them accessed without the benefit of a platform. Double doors came together in the middle of each car and very high up in the corners were two tiny grated rectangles. This was the only space air and light could enter the cars once the doors were shut.

Wagons, sleighs, carts and some trucks arrived carrying those to be deported and their belongings. Under heavy armed guard the prisoners were crowded into the vehicles. They stood packed together, hugging each other and their bundles. The soldiers herded them toward the train and prodded them along like cattle with the ends of their bayonets.

The tops of the boxcars were covered with white mounds of snow. Some of the doors were already shut and bolted; in the bitter frosty air the stench was overwhelming. The trains, after being loaded, often stood for days before leaving. The tracks along which they stood soon became piled with human excrement and urine. It ran under the cars onto the tracks and down the embankments. The ground soon became boggy, trampled and foul.

The frightening silhouettes of the NKVD soldiers stood out against the white snow. Immense crowds of onlookers swayed in and out;, the soldiers forced them back, all except those they shoved toward the boxcars.

Children were torn from their mother's grasp; older people stumbled. Families became separated as they were pushed into one part of the train while their loved ones were pushed into another. When the doors shut the light went with it. The interior was cramped; they struggled to sort themselves out, find space for their belongings.

Someone climbed on the ledge by the rectangular window and gave a blow by blow description of what was happening outside.

When the trains finally moved out life settled into one of survival. There was a stove in the middle of each car; someone cut a hole in the corner of the floor and if there was a blanket to spare it was draped around it to give some privacy. They slept on the shelves that ran along the top packed together like sardines. The smoke from the stove added to the foul air, as did the unwashed bodies and stale breath.

Since the railroad tracks were also used by military transports their cars were often side railed, sometimes for days. On some trains, once a day soldiers would open the doors and pass in a kettle of watery soup and a loaf of stale bread. Every few days, under armed guard, one car at a time would be allowed to get out and walk around in a confined space. There were always soldiers with rifles and bayonets.

There was no sharing among the passengers. Soon even those who had brought food with them ran out. All the cars had one passenger in common, his name was death. First the very old and the very young died, then the sickly and those who lost all hope. When the trains stopped on a siding the dead were thrown off the cars onto the frozen earth.

When they first got on the train most of the Poles were healthy and still able to put up a fight. Now their existence was one of survival. Cold, hunger, thirst, lice infestation, foul air, dirt and diarrhea took their toll. People succumbed in stages, some suffered more, some less depending on what the Russian soldiers allowed them to bring.

Regina's Tale - flight from Siberia

All in all it added up to death for many, torment for some and mere discomfort for a very few.

Ten year old Regina and her family struggled in their car to keep warm, eating the millet her father had brought with them. Her small frame, healthy and strong at the beginning of the trip had little excess fat to spare. She huddled with her two younger brothers and waited, as did everyone else, to find out what was to become of her.

Sometimes the person looking out of the window would call out a name of a town as the train passed. In this way they knew where they were and what direction the train was going. Other times the sights seen were not passed on: a young woman holding a baby was being herded toward one of the cars by a soldier, she thrust her baby into the arms of an onlooker. The other woman cradled the baby and started to run away from the train. A soldier aimed and fired, the woman and baby fell to the ground.

Hunger, fright and smoke filled the interior of the car while bugs and lice began to infest their bodies. They slept fitfully on the hard shelves.

After a journey of thirty days the train stopped for the last time. When the doors were flung open they found they were in Kotlas, Siberia.

5 KOTLAS, SIBERIA 1940

We arrived at Kotlas, Siberia in March; they put us on sleds, it took us two days to get to camp. We had to cross over the river Dwina. It was still winter, the snow was very deep and it was very cold, forty degrees below zero. Sled was the only transportation. In the summer time you could take a paddle boat.

They took us to a big barracks built with logs with moss between. There was one entrance, a hallway and four rooms. So one room to a family, on the end was a bathroom, once a week a guy would come and scoop up from there and throw it out. There was one well for all that camp.

It was one village, hundreds of barracks, eight families to some, like a duplex four by four. Each had a wood stove, built in oven with bricks for heat and for cooking. Wood bunks, lots of wood.

There were some people already living there that were deported from the first war from Belarus. They thought they would never get out.

The commandant had said to them 'You will get out from here when hair will grow on my hand.'

The village was surrounded by forest, there were no guards. Everyone had to work in the forest if you were over fifteen years old, but my mother didn't have to go, she was allowed to stay with our family. There was no place to go, the forest was all around, hardly anyone escaped because of the wolves in the forest. It was two days by river to Rabova over ten kilometers of poor country roads. There were three months of summer, nine months of winter. In the middle of the village was a well with a pail on a rope. Ice never melted on the water, used a pick to get water, crack the ice. One day a neighbor asked me to get her a pail of water. The pail sat on the edge of the well, it fell into the well with the rope, I finally got it back.

We children went to school, I had to repeat the second grade because I couldn't speak Russian. They gave us a book, I was so afraid because we poked

Stalin's eyes out with our pens then we had to give the book back. We had to cover it up somehow. There was one boy, he was fifteen with red hair and freckles. He was in the second grade, they wouldn't pass him, he was very slow.

We had in the beginning whatever extra clothes we could bring. We exchanged them for bag of potatoes. In the spring they gave us parcels.

We had to remove stems and plant potatoes and cabbage. In the fall we found mushrooms.

My father was a lumberjack, he was an expert on wood so he would mark the trees, which one would be good to cut. They were cutting lots of birch for guns.

In summer we were allowed to plant our own garden, still we didn't get enough vitamins. My father get blindness, chicken blindness. He can't see anything after sunset so they sent him to cut wood for the hospital. He had a big saw but he couldn't do it by himself so he took me to pull that thing so it would saw the wood. I had to pull it, he could pull it himself but I kept it straight.

One day the teacher came 'So how come she's not in school?'

I had a dress, didn't have pants, with a yoke and every time I was pulling the saw it caught on my dress. My dress was in strips.

My father said, 'She had nothing to wear, look at her.' The teacher gave up and left, didn't bother us again.

My father always knew what was going on, he was very political. The commandant came one day, he said there was amnesty and said, 'You're free to leave.'

They gave a piece of paper so we could travel. In July of 1941 my father was rushing everything because by September the river would be frozen. He wanted to go across the river by paddle boat, you can take thirty five people at a time.

My father said, 'I don't trust Stalin because he was Russian.' We were lucky ones, we get out, but not everyone got out because Stalin woke up and said 'No more.'

He stopped others from leaving. We left in August, across the Dwina river.

How it started, Polish general in government-in-exile in London, General Sirkorski went to Stalin when Hitler hit the Russians. He said, 'You have so many of my people in the east in Gulag,' there was millions of us taken. He said, 'Let my people go and we'll fight with you,' and that's why we got amnesty.

The general of the others in charge of the Polish army said they were going south to Uzbekistan. North was the north pole, east was German and there was war with Germany and west was Hitler, the only way we could go was South.

Siberia is a land of snow, howling wolves, forest and salt mines. Rasputin was born there, Lenin exiled there, Maxim Gorky called it a land of chains and ice. Kotlas, Russia was a special place on the map of Siberia. Not only did the railroad line end there but it was almost a Polish village. It was already populated by a large number of Polish exiles from the Ukraine who had been displaced and sent there from the 1910's and 1920's.

When the box car doors opened the deportees saw huge mounds of snow and a row of sleighs harnessed with local Siberian ponies. Bodies wasted by starvation, close quarters and foul air had to be 'helped' off the train. Stumbling, carrying what possessions they had they were herded onto sleds and barges. Prisoners were taken from Kotlas into the vast expanses of the Archangel and Komi Taiga, a region which was literally sprinkled with involuntary work camps. From here the prisoners headed in the direction of the White Sea, the Barents Sea and Vorkuta.

They traveled further north stopping only to rest the ponies. Finally there was a large lake, the Dwnia river; they made the crossing on the frozen surface toward a village on the farther side. They were taken to camp #122, Tiesowaja.

Approximately 138 slave labor camps were in the Archangel Taiga. The region covers 365,000 square miles of forests. Deep, dark, dense forests from which the Russians harvested lumber. Huge trees growing close together cast deep shadows on the land. Their trunks were as large as table tops in girth and you could hardly see their tops. Working with hand tools, axes, two man saws, the inhabitants of the camps were forced to work up to fourteen hours a day felling trees. In extreme weather they stripped bark, cleared brush, dug the frozen ground with pix axes and moved logs down the Dwnia river. It was dangerous exhausting work which only became worse as starvation and sickness invaded their bodies.

As they arrived the families were lined up in front of a row of wooden barracks and the commandant gave his speech.

'This is not a holiday camp, you are here to work for the greater glory of the Soviet Union and the Revolution. You will earn your food by working. Remember, he who does not work, does not eat.'

As each family was assigned to a barracks, they dragged their belongings with them. Inside, crudely constructed wooden bunk beds with thick straw-filled mattresses lined the rooms. In one corner was a small brick stove. As the occupants went about unpacking their meager supplies their captors prepared the evening meal, a thin hot soup with a small piece of brown bread.

Everyone over the age of fifteen was required to work in the forests. Ann was allowed to stay with her family, still Regina at the age of ten would watch over and care for her two younger brothers.

The camp already had Polish inhabitants who had been exiled there in 1910 during the first world war. They had never been allowed to leave. They had made their homes in the area and raised their families. The school had Russian teachers and the hospital Russian Doctors and nurses.

The children were sent to school every day. Regina had to repeat the second grade as she didn't speak any Russian.

'Truancy won't be tolerated,' the head teacher told them, 'your parents will be responsible for your attendance, they will be severely punished for all your transgressions.'

Finally she told them that the adults would be given their rations at work and the children would be fed at school.

Women were expected to do the work of men, cutting down trees, chopping branches off felled logs. They were told, 'If you don't work, you don't eat. If you want a full ration and something to take home to your children you must do the work of a man. Lighter tasks mean smaller rewards.'

If outcome fell short of the 'norm' set by the Commandant their income was reduced accordingly. From that money the administrators deducted the cost of food dished out to them as well as to their children. Of course the earnings didn't cover the cost of basic food and families soon fell into debt. They couldn't afford the luxury of falling ill.

But hunger, cold and intense labor led to malnutrition, scurvy, and in Regina's case pellagra and dysentery. Because there were no green vegetables, meat, eggs or seafood, vitamin B was lacking from their diet. Pellagra caused severe diarrhea, weakness and sometimes nervous disorders. Dysentery, also known as Bloody Flux, occurred from inflamed intestines caused by contaminated food or water. It manifested in bloody diarrhea, fever and abdomen pain. All of this led to weakness, malnutrition and often death.

Stefan came down with 'chicken blindness' (night blindness) the inability to see at night. This also was caused by a lack of vitamins, especially Vitamin A.

He could no longer work as an expert forester marking the trees to be cut. Instead he was sent to cut wood for the hospital. Unable to work alone, weakened by malnutrition, he took Regina out of school to help him.

Hunger, hard work and malnutrition also took its toll on Ann, who was now pregnant.

Despite the harshness of the camps some of the children and a few adults made crude skates from wood and wire. They used them to skate on the frozen river. In this way, adventurous young men went to other encampments trading news and whatever belongings they still had.

Russian villages were also in the area, and the poor peasants were all too eager to trade food from their meager supply for the clothes and keepsakes the Poles had brought with them. They were far nicer than anything the Russians possessed.

The dreary harsh life of the camp was broken with news of the war. When the Poles first arrived they were encouraged to write letters home to relatives or friends left behind and ask for supplies. The letters were heavily censored, but still word spread.

Clandestine meetings between the men kept Stefan aware of events that would directly affect him and his family.

In the spring, each family was given a small plot of land for a garden. The soil was poor and the growing season short. Seeds bought from the Russian supply store were of poor quality and the saved potatoes barely had time to grow. Berries and mushrooms were gathered from the forests and put aside for the winter. It was a daily struggle of survival.

There was never enough food and what there was, was of poor quality lacking needed vitamins and minerals.

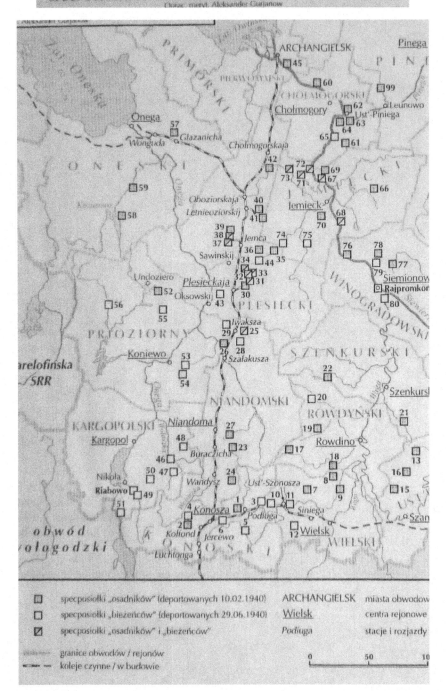

Kotlas, Siberia Camp #122, Tiesowaja

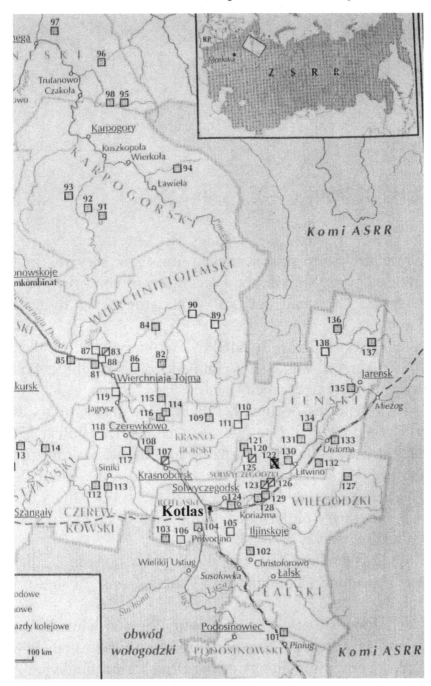

6 POLISH GOVERNMENT-IN-EXILE

While the Siminskis scratched for their survival in the labor camp of Siberia, the Polish government-in-exile was at work. They had not, nor would they ever forget the deportees.

When Poland was invaded by Germany in September of 1939 General Wladyslaw Sikorski, one of three Polish Prime ministers, escaped to Paris.

It's territories occupied, Poland as a free country was still recognized by the Western Allies. The Polish Navy had already sailed to Britain and thousands of troops escaped via Romania, Hungary or across the Baltic Sea. Those routes would be used until the end of the war by both interned soldiers and volunteers from Poland, who called themselves 'Sikorski's tourists.'

On November 7th General Sikorski, now in England, was appointed Commander in Chief of the Polish Armed Forces.

On June 19, 1940 he met with Winston Churchill, the Prime Minister of England, and promised that Polish forces would fight alongside the British until final victory.

One year later on June 22, 1941 without warning Hitler broke his pact with Stalin and attacked the whole of the new Russian-German border.

Stalin quickly switched allegiances and joined Great Britain to form a united front against Germany.

When Hitler invaded Russia General Sikorski saw his chance. Stalin, as a price for joining the Alliance, demanded military and material assistance to resist the Germans. General Sikorski knew that when the Russian Red Army invaded Eastern Poland in 1939 over 200,000 Polish soldiers were taken as prisoners. Officers and enlisted men were transferred to prisoner of war camps then exiled along with hundreds of thousands of Polish civilians to the harsh lands of Siberia. There they were forced to work in the forests and mines as slave laborers. Among the soldiers were thousands from the Kresy Region of Eastern Poland. One of their Generals, Wladyslaw Anders, had been sent to the Lubyanka Prison in Russia. A prison famous for torture and death.

As a member of the British delegation to Russia General Sikorski requested a meeting with Joseph Stalin.

'Marshal, I hear you are making demands for the British to come to your aid,' Sikorski began. 'Their human resources are limited, you may find yourself disappointed.' He paused then said 'I think I have a solution.'

'Who do you think hates the Germans the most?' General Sikorski continued.

Stalin appeared puzzled so Sikorski answered. 'Why, the Poles of course. How many good Polish fighting men do you have in your prison camps? I think these people, properly trained and equipped, could make a much bigger contribution defeating the Germans than digging salt in the mines of the Ural Mountains or felling trees in Siberia.'

He then laid out a plan to Stalin, 'You demand that the Allies have those people cross the border to Persia or Iraq. There they are to be fed and clothed and generally prepared for war by the British. Once the units are ready to fight you can demand they be brought back to face your enemy. This whole business won't cost you a penny and the Allies will be glad to get you off their backs. Remember, they are short of fighting men not food or equipment.'

Stalin was a dictator and ruled his county with an iron fist. He knew this would give him fighting men under the control of Russia's Red Army. He mulled the proposal over, 'I can't see anything wrong with it, those Polish dogs would certainly fight the Germans more fiercely than anyone I know.' He smiled and roared, 'Sergeant, bring a bottle of good Polish vodka immediately. My friend General Sikorski and I have an agreement to seal.'

7 AMNESTY

The Polish general in exile in London went to Stalin when Hitler hit Russia. He said, you have so many of my people from the East of Poland, there was millions of us taken. He said let my people go and we'll fight with you. And that's why we got amnesty. Otherwise we probably be dead.

The general in charge of the Polish army said, 'I don't trust the Russians, that's why we are traveling to Persia.' They were going South to Uzbekistan.

North was North Pole, East was Germans, West was Hitler; the only way we could go was South. The Shah of Iran was still in good with England and he said, 'I'll give you transit.'

They knew in Uzbekistan that the Polish Army was organizing there and the civilians were going to it. My father knew we had to leave, he didn't trust Stalin. He got our papers, he wanted to leave before September when the River would start to freeze over. We took a paddle boat over the water.

My father sold everything to get tickets for the train. My mother was pregnant and couldn't go with us. My father took her to the hospital in Kotlas, she stayed behind to have the baby.

We left the camp and made our way to Samarkand.

The fate of Polish exiles was completely changed in June of 1941. The Soviet authorities issued a decree announcing an amnesty for all Poles currently on Soviet soil. It was an astounding event, never before had the enforced laborers been set free.

In the labor camps each Commandant gathered all the adult population and read the Decree out loud. After, he looked up and waited for a response. When none came he added, 'As of today you are all free people. Papers to that effect will be issued to each family. This means you will be able to go wherever and whenever you please. If any official tries to stop you show them your papers.'

The adults were stunned, 'As you know, the Germans now occupy your country so don't go back to Poland. On top of this we have no facilities to transport you away from here.'

Then the commandant tried to convince the people to stay and build houses. He told them their pay would be doubled. If they insisted on leaving he reminded them transport would have to be arranged and it might be some time before this could be done.

However provisions had also been made for the creation of an army from these newly-freed prisoners. General Wladyslaw Anders, who had been interred in the Lubyanka prison in Moscow, was to be its commander. Stalin intended to mobilize this new army immediately in his fight with Germany. They would be formed into the Polish regiment under the control of the Russian Red Army.

General Anders persuaded him to hold back, to let the recently released Poles regain their strength.

The Poles intended that not just the men got out of the camps but as many of their people, women and children as possible, would leave.

The gathering dispersed, it was all too much to absorb. The notion of staying was out of the question. 'Where to go?' they would ask. After some days of discussion, groups were to go to the Commandant's office and register their chosen destination. Again they were told arrangements for travel would be up to them, they could go anywhere but they would have to find the way.

The food improved, somewhat, the pay was better, still not enough, but as weeks passed the occupants of the camp started to get impatient.

Ever since the winter the effects of malnutrition, cold, exhaustion and poor hygiene were becoming more apparent. It started with chills followed by persistent coughs. Later, diarrhea, Tuberculosis, Dysentery, Night Blindness and other severe illnesses set in.

In spite of the improved conditions the death toll was accelerating.

Regina and her family had been in the labor camp for eighteen months. Her father sold what possessions they had left and gathered enough money to get them onto a train.

8 SAMARKAND, UZBEKISTAN

We went onto a Russian train, in boxcars. It was not a regular train and there was only one set of tracks so when another train came we were put to the side to wait till we could go again. We knew we were hungry, badly hungry. If you had a mother, well she could always find something but a father... I was sickly, had dysentery and couldn't eat. I remember women on the train would get something and cook it up. There were quite a few in the boxcar, we were very hungry. Everyone had free pass, could go anywhere.

Never knew how long train would stay there, could be couple days or a week. Couldn't go to town. It was fall and the fields had been worked, lots of potatoes. When the train stopped the doors would be open and people would sit on the floor looking out, they could see the fields and where some of the potatoes were. Sometimes people would get off the train to get potatoes or something. When they came back the train would be gone. That's how people got lost, families got separated.

The Polish army was organizing in Bukhara, it was under British command; they fed, clothed and trained the men.

As we traveled through Uzbekistan whenever we stopped at a town there were Polish soldiers wearing army uniforms supplied by the British with a Polish Insignia on their arm. They took the children who had no family, orphans without parents, and took them to a local orphanage.

We were on the train for a month. Once we were side railed when other trains passed, we got off the train in Tashkent and we were taken to a large hall where we were served chicken noodle soup. Just ate then went back to the train.

The part of the world that brings to mind the Tales of Saharazard or Alladin and his lamp was as different from the dark cold forests of Siberia as night is to day. Once a major city on the Silk Route from China to the West, Samarkand was described in 1333 by Moor Abu Abdullah

Ibn Battuta as 'One of the largest and most perfectly beautiful cities in the world.'

From the first century BC the Silk Route was a network of interlinking trade routes across Afro Eurasia that connected East, South and Western Asia as well as parts of North and East Africa with the Mediterranean and the European world. Caravans of camels and mules brought to China dates, saffron powder and pistachio nuts. Frankincense, aloes and myrrh came from Somnalia. Sandalwood came from India and glass bottles from Egypt. Returning caravans brought back bolts of silk brocade, lacquer ware and porcelain.

Not just goods but ideas and culture were interchanged, Zoroastrianism, Judaism, Buddhism, Christianity, Manichaeism and Islam. Samarkand became a city of mosques, temples and churches. Pungent spices, rare dyes, exotic fruits were available in her markets as well as leather, precious stones, melons, grapes and a host of other goods.

It's diverse population included Turks, Hindus, Jews and Christians.

Marco Polo was one of the first Europeans to travel the Silk route to China and write about his adventures. In turn the devastating "Black Death" also traveled it in 1340's to Europe.

Then in 1868 the country of Uzbekistan of which Samarkand was then the capital, was captured by the Russians and became part of the Soviet empire.

In 1941 when Stalin gave the Poles their freedom, a mass exodus began from the frozen forests of Siberia and the mines of Russian provinces. They headed for the army reception camps in Tashkent (the current capital of Uzbekistan), Kermine, Samarkand and Ashkaband, where the Polish army was being organized. Stalin wanted only the men to be released so they could be trained to fight with the Russians against the Germans.

Instead thousands of civilians left the Gulag system. Women and children began a desperate journey, some on foot, to reach reception camps on the borders of Iran and Afghanistan. Some existed on a diet of pancakes made from wheat chaff and pig weed, others on whatever they could scavenge.

They traveled thousands of miles, an exodus of hundreds of thousands under terrible conditions. Many froze to death or starved. Others kept themselves alive by selling whatever personal objects they still had. Exhausted mothers, unable to walk any further, placed their children into the arms of strangers.

When they arrived at the army reception camps the refugees tried to enlist in the Polish Army. The Soviets had allocated some food and provisions but there was nothing for the hoards of hungry women and children who camped outside the military bases. The Polish army enlisted as many of the civilians as they could, including children (regardless of age or sex) to save them from starvation. Communal graves in Uzbekistan could not keep up with the numbers who died. By 1942, only half of the 1.7 million Polish citizens arrested by Russians in 1940 were still alive.

Samarkand, one of the greenest cities of Uzbekistan, was filled with plantations of fruit and decorative trees, flower gardens and pools. The median temperature is 90°F (32°C) and during the summer well over 100°F (38°C). The city was totally unprepared for the amount of refugees that began to arrive, some by foot, many by train. They were dirty, lice ridden and skeletal, starved for food and self esteem.

9 KOLKHOZ

We went through Samarkand, there was my father, brother Edmund, older sister Irene, me and my younger brothers, Zenon and Jan. We stayed on a kolkhoz, a collective farm, while picking cotton. They gave us a room in a house, sometimes four to five families to one room. We moved constantly, they were collective farms, a government official would come and get workers and take them in a two wheeled cart pulled by a donkey. I was eleven so didn't pick cotton, was babysitting my two younger brothers.

We crossed the AmuDarya river in Uzbekistan to another kolkhoz. We traveled in a grain barge, it had only a big hole where the grain would go. We were in there, in the hole, my brothers would run around on top, there were no rails, I was afraid they would fall off.

The people would harvest cotton on different farms. We would go to Turtkul to pick cotton then return to Samarkand. In Samarkand were lots of orchards, tropical fruit, grapes. Cherry, apricot orchards, the hyenas were in there at night and lots of people had dysentery so couldn't eat the fruit, Watermelon was the worst.

I saw things I never saw in Poland; surprised to see quilted jackets, people who wore thick felt on their feet - they made shoes from birch bark to protect their slippers. Saw Tartars, women who had pants they wore like a dress with pillbox on their heads. Lots of beads, the men were in skirts.

In Persia they dressed differently, in India they wore saris. Such a shock seeing earrings in nose and ears. The Hindus had little darker skin, Tartars I had seen them before, a little bit I saw in Poland, they were always fighting in Poland. Saw my first black person in Bombay, he was working at the railroad station.

One day when we were at a kolkhoz my older brother and his friend killed a sheep. It was forbidden to kill a sheep. They wrapped the skin in a stone and threw it into the river. Wild dogs dragged it out of the water onto shore and the police found it. They came to the house and saw me and the other children gnawing on bones. They accused my brother of killing the sheep. They were going to arrest him. My father told them he had gone into Samarkand and bought the meat, so they let my brother go.

After that my brother joined the Polish army and I never saw him until we were in England.

On steppes of grass sheep grazed, my little brothers and I caught little green turtles the size of a saucer. I carried them in a sack on my back, could feel them moving. I killed them, took a rock and split them open, that was all the meat we had, we ate a lot of turtles.

In the bigger towns the people were supposed to give bread or something to eat. Once we lived in a house with friend of my father's. He knew him from Poland, the friend had been transported in WW I and was working in a big house. We stayed with him for a while. There was never enough to eat.

Conditions were so hard. Irene, my older sister, was only fourteen. She and my father left to join the army, she joined the youth corps, anything just to get out of our conditions. Before my father joined the Polish army he gave me and my two younger brothers to the orphanage in Kattakurgan, Uzbekistan. The orphanage wouldn't take Irene because she was too old. Fourteen year old was supposed to work. So my father put her in youth corp.

There were eighty six kids, we stayed there until there was a transport train. The Polish government-in-exile heard that Stalin was going to rescind amnesty, they wanted to get the Poles out of Russia.

They emptied the orphanage. The guardian pulled me along by my arm. I was so sick. We were taken to the port of Krashowodsk on the Caspian Sea. We were put on a boat. A boat that held one hundred people now had eight hundred.

We were on the second to the last ship to go, they put so many people on the boat

The ship was swaying to one side. I slept with my two brothers, one foot space, we stayed together in small space. There was no water, no toilet only a blanket over a pail. It took three days.

My father tried to see my mother who was in hospital in Krashowdsk, she was supposed to be there but she was already gone, transferred to Tehran, Iran.

When Josef Stalin launched his 'revolution' in 1927 he set two goals for Soviet domestic policy. Rapid industrialization and collectivization of agriculture. He wanted to erase capitalism and transform the Soviet Union into a completely socialist state.

The first of his five year plans was to industrialize the economy with emphasis on heavy industry. By 1940, ninety seven percent of all peasant households had been collectivized. Private ownership of property was almost eliminated.

As many as one hundred families were stripped of property rights to form one collective called a Kolkhoz. It was divided into work units with brigades. The head, called the brigadier, was usually a local man who was equipped with draught horses for the people to work the land.

Members of the kolkhoz were paid a share of the farm's product, only one third of them received cash for their work. They were required to sell their crop to the state with fixed prices. Members could hold small areas of private land and a few animals but this was usually under an acre.

They were required to do a minimum number of days at work each year on both the farms and government work projects such as road building.

Into this oppressive atmosphere, hundreds of thousands of Polish refugees now appeared looking for work.

Uzbekistan was neighbor to Turkmenistan and Kazakhstan which border the Caspian Sea. The terrain is mountainous, as well as desert and expanses of steppes.

The steppes are grassland plains with few trees. It is a semi-arid land with extreme ranges in temperatures from 104°F to -40°F (40°C to -40°C). Cotton was the major crop, planted on the land of the kolkhoz'.

The vast majority of the refugees were sent to various kolkhozes to pick cotton. They would earn meager wages in the hot climate. To supplement their pay many would then walk kilometers to find a Polish relief organization. These groups were established and funded by the Polish government-in-exile and would supply needed food and clothes. They did this until their funding ran out.

Eventually the cotton ran out too, the harvest was over, there was no more work.

Stefan and his oldest son worked the fields taking the younger children along when they traveled to other kolkoz'. When there wasn't any more work he had to come up with another plan. He put the younger children into an orphanage, Irene joined the youth corps and he joined the Polish army.

10 STALIN RESINDS AMNESTY

Regina's father knew that Stalin wasn't to be trusted. When the amnesty came he managed to get his children out of Siberia and his wife into a hospital in Kotlas. Ann was pregnant and very ill, unable to travel with them.

But they weren't to be free for very long. When the amnesty was rescinded by Stalin few knew the real reason, only that they had to get off of Soviet controlled territory or be sent back to Siberia.

So why did Stalin 'wake up' and say 'no more'?

Katyn Forest Massacre

In 1941, on their push against the Soviets, German troops had taken over the area of the Katyn Forest located near Smolonsk in Western Russia. What they found in the forest gave them, they thought, a tool to use to drive a wedge between the Soviet Union and the Western Allies. So they took several American and British Prisoners of War out of their prison camps and into the forest.

Regina's Tale - flight from Siberia

The POW's were horrified when they were shown the unearthed mass graves. Thousands upon thousands of corpses clothed in Polish Military Officers uniforms lay in the now open ground. They had been massacred.

Stalin claimed that the atrocity had been carried out by the Germans. When General Sikorski refused to accept this explanation and requested it be investigated by the International Red Cross, the Soviets accused the Polish government-in-exile of cooperating with Nazi Germany. They refused to give permission for the Red Cross to investigate the allegation.

Six years after the war ended, on September 18, 1951, the United States House of Representatives established a committee to investigate the Katyn Massacre, which was considered an international crime committed against Polish soldiers of WW II. The members of the United States committee included Thaddeus M. Michrowicz, a Democrat from Michigan.

This massacre involved over 4,243 of the 15,400 Polish Army officers who were captured by the Soviets when Russia invaded Poland in 1939.

These officers had been interned in three prison camps in the U.S.S.R.. At first, they had been allowed to write letters home, but in May of 1940 the letters stopped. All trace of these men was lost. No further communication was heard; nothing further of their whereabouts was known until the mass graves were found in the forest of Katyn in April of 1943.

It was one of the most barbarous international crimes in the world. The Soviets blamed the Germans, they charged the Poles had fallen into Nazi hands.

However the Germans organized a medical commission consisting of doctors from twelve European nations. They met at Katyn on April 28th and 29th of 1943 and unanimously determined that the Poles were massacred in the spring of 1940. At that time the Katyn area was under the complete domination of the Soviets.

The flower of Polish military and Polish society, over four thousand officers had been executed by Stalin in order to destroy any Polish capacity for resisting Russian occupation of their country after the war. The evidence was unimpeachable, the bodies had been dead for many months in an area Germany had only recently occupied.

Polish soldiers had been taken from Russian Prisoner of War camps by trucks. They were marched down a path through the dark forest to a clearing. Arms tied behind their backs, pushed to the rim of a mass grave, and executed. Their bodies were pushed over the edge to land on top of already dead comrades, they lay like cords of wood layer upon layer. When the German disinterred the bodies they found the cold Russian soil had delayed decomposition. Rifling through their uniforms they found pictures, wallets and in one case a diary. In it the Polish officer had kept a daily journal, the last entry read, 'they are taking us into a forest.'

The American and British POW's who were taken to the forest to view the graves were allowed to get messages back to their countrymen about the massacre. But, Winston Churchill, Prime Minister of Britain, and President Roosevelt of the United States kept the massacre hidden from the public for military expediency. In keeping it secret the true nature of the communist leaders was also kept secret. By the time the truth was known Poland was already under Soviet control.

In the summer of 1941 when Stalin released Polish prisoners to form a fighting unit under the direction of the

Red Army, high-level Polish officials tried to obtain information regarding the missing officers.

The Soviets claimed no knowledge and refused to cooperate either with the Poles or the United States in trying to locate them. The Russians felt the United States was intervening in Russo-Polish problems.

Fearing Russia might make a separate peace with the Germans, the United States took a gamble on Russia's pledge to work with the Western democracies after the war. President Roosevelt refused to believe that the Soviets were responsible for the Katyn massacre.

It was obvious the President and the State Department ignored documents presented to them due to their desire for mutual cooperation with Russia in the war effort. The American foreign policy called for a free post war Poland; they also wanted a Polish army in the Near East to help fight the war.

The Russians had plotted to take over Poland as early as 1939. The massacre of the Polish officers was designed to eliminate the intellectual leadership which would have attempted to block communization of their country.

The discovery of the mass graves and the following investigation gave the Soviets a reason to break off relations with Poland. When this happened the Polish government-in-exile tried to get as many Poles off of Soviet held territories as possible.

Ships left the port of Krasnovodsk, Turkmenistan overloaded with refugees. Regina and her brothers were on the second to last boat that left.

People were throwing themselves into the water trying to get onto the last ship that left the port. Those that stayed behind faced an uncertain future. They would now be considered Russian citizens.

The ships that successfully made the journey carried the Polish women and children across the Caspian sea to Tehran.

11 PAHLAVI, IRAN

The summer of 1942 thousands of soldiers and civilians were in transports from Krasnovadsk on the Caspian Sea. Over a million Poles remained in Soviet Union, on the last transport people were packed on board in coal holds. Polish soldiers started to remove possession and throw them overboard so more people would fit.

The sea was oil polluted, very dirty, it was very hot, no water. I had dysentery and pellagra, matter of fact, we were so weak we had to walk a few miles to the railroad station in KattaKurgan to get to Krasnovodsk, the guardian of us, from the orphanage, she had to drag me because I couldn't walk.

People were so weak coming off the boat, soldiers had to help them. When we came to Pahlavi I was running and there was a tent camp. It was so hot, you could throw a egg on the sand and you have boiled egg in no time.

I had no shoes, no underwear, no nothing. Just had a dress and they took me to, like a MASH hospital in a tent.

There was a dirty and clean area, the dirty area was for people with lice, bugs. An orderly washed me and burned my clothes and shaved my head, he gave me a clean gown. He recognized my name and asked me if I knew Ann Siminski? I said, she's my mother, he told me she had been admitted in the morning and transferred to a hospital in Tehran, I was admitted in the afternoon. We just missed each other. I did not see my mother, she had a baby girl on the train out of Kotlas and she (the baby) died, it was probably thrown off the train because that is what they did.

I was in the Polish hospital for six weeks, sick for three years. Nobody ever came. I was used to being alone, had to be tough to survive.

There was nine kids in my tent, four beds on one side then other with nursing station. I was in bed four. One day, it was dark yet, they carry one boy out half hour later they carry another boy out. Daybreak took another boy out. I was in fourth bed, I was pinching myself because I didn't know when I was going to die. Because those three boys, all dead, were carried out. When was it my turn?

They cured me from dysentery, strict diet for six weeks. Porridge was boiled for hours then strained through a cheese cloth. I drank the liquid. Then I had mashed potatoes and finally released.

On the shores of the Caspian Sea there were hastily constructed camp of tents and open shelters. Very large tents and thatched roof stalls, we slept on the sand. There was so much food, after two years couldn't believe it.

My father had Malaria so was discharged from army he got us out of orphanage and got Irene out of the youth camp for girls.

The evacuation of Polish nationals from the Soviet Union took place by sea from Krasnovodsk to Pahlavi and overland from Ashkabad to Mashhad. Between March 24 and August 30 of 1942 115,000 people were evacuated, 37,000 of them were civilians, 18,000 children (only seven percent of the number of Polish citizens originally exiled to the Soviet Union.)

A makeshift city comprising over 2,000 tents was erected along the shoreline of Pahlavi to accommodate the refugees. It stretched for miles, a vast complex of bathhouses, latrines, disinfection booths, laundries, sleeping quarters, bakeries and a hospital. Every unoccupied house in the city was requisitioned, every chair appropriated from local cinemas. Still it was inadequate.

The Iranian and British officials who first watched the Soviet oil tankers and coal ships list into the harbor at Pahlavi had little idea how many people to expect or what physical state they might be in. Only a few days earlier they were alarmed to hear that civilians, women and children were to be included, they were totally unprepared.

The ships from Krasnovodsk were grossly overcrowded. Every available space on board was filled. Some passengers were little more than walking skeletons covered in rags and lice. The boats and small ships were vessels of hope but for some they were bearers of death. Many began to die from typhoid and other diseases.

2,806 refugees died within a few months of arriving in Iran. Row upon row of tombstones line a Roman Catholic cemetery in a poor neighborhood of Tehran. Etched on them is a single year of death: 1942. Regina's mother Ann is buried there.

Weakened by two years of starvation hard labor and disease they were suffering from exhaustion, dysentery, malaria, typhus, skin infections, chicken blindness and itching scabs.

An infected area and a clean area of the camp was allocated. Infectious diseases were quarantined or sent to the camp hospital. At this time there were only ten doctors and twenty five nurses in the whole of Pahlavi.

There were three major camps in Tehran, all primitive, each had an orphanage. There were outbreaks of Typhus and typhoid fever.

In the clean area arrivals had their clothes collected and burned. They were showered, deloused and some had their heads shaved. Women began to wear head scarves to conceal their baldness. Finally they were given sheets, blankets and fresh clothes by the Red Cross. Polish organizations in America had collected clothing and donated it. Boys found themselves wearing girls combinations, some women were given night dresses or men's pj's.

Over 18,000 children of all ages and sex (mostly girls) arrived at Pahlavi. Some had been separated from their families during the long journey through Russia. Many were painfully emaciated and malnourished. Orphanages were set up in Pahlavi, Tehran and Ahvaz.

Iranian civil authorities and private individuals vacated premises to accommodate the children. Schools, hospital and social organizations sprang up all over the city. The new Shah took especial interest in the Polish children of Isfahan. He allowed them the use of his swimming pool, invited groups of them to his palace for dinner. In time, some of the children began to learn Farsi. At its peak, twenty-four areas of the city were allocated to the orphans. As a result, Isfahan became known ever after in Polish émigré circles as the City of Polish Children.

The refugees remained in Pahlavi for a period of a few days to several months before being transferred to other more permanent camps in Tehran, Mashhad and Ahvaz.

Lorries carried some of the evacuees to Tehran. It was a beautiful drive through forests until you got to the mountains with hairpin turns, then suddenly you were in the desert again in tents sleeping on the sand.

12 TEHRAN, IRAN

I was in Hospital for three months, a British hospital, a regular hospital in a building. In 1943 was still having recurring fevers. An old priest came to give me Communion, he had tears in his eyes. I said I don't know how to confess. I had only gone once when I made my First Communion in my village.

Father came to see me. He met a Jewish Doctor in the hall. Father had bananas, oranges, the Doctor asked him 'Who are you going to see?' Then he said 'Give it to her if you want to see her dead.' I was in a separate room, by myself, saw my father standing by my door trying not to cry, had tears in his eyes.

They didn't have vitamins so they gave me calf liver with onion and salt and pepper, had to swallow raw two tablespoons every day. My Doctor in Cadillac told me that probably saved my life and they still use that in the Philippines today.

I was discharged, there were six different camps, brothers, father and sister were in camp #3. Bus dropped me off in camp, I could eat anything, was very hungry. In a big tent, quite a few people, somebody scrambled eggs and I ate all of them. They thought I would get sick.

We lived in American barracks, cement with cement floors, used them as stables but now they were clean. We were sleeping like sardines with only a middle pass way. The Americans had dances, lots of war brides met their husbands there.

My father met a woman there, he liked her because she took good care of her sons.

Father was recalled into army and was sent to Palestine. He was in his fifties by then. We had no documents so you could say anything you want. He told them he was born in 1899. He was in till the end of the war.

He sent us back to an orphanage in Ahwaz. This time Irene was allowed to go with us, there wasn't an age limit. After one or two month we went to the Gulf of Persia to Karachi, Pakistan. Stayed three months in hospital in

Karachi. British hospital built for British citizens. Doctors were mostly English with a translator. One Doctor from America who was Polish. They wanted to do surgery for my tonsils. They told me I needed surgery on my tonsils, that they would burn my tonsils out. Very scared, all alone, didn't understand they were going to do cryonic surgery. I was supposed to have seven treatments but had only three.

We thought we would go back to Poland. We were supposed to go to Africa but because I was so sick I went to India, first to Bombay then Valiverde. I was going to Sanatorium and Irene, Zenon and Jan were supposed to go to Africa. Father wrote a letter to the commandant of the camp 'Don't separate the children.'

We all went to Karachi then Mumbai where I was sent to the Panchgani Sanatorium in the mountains in Khalapur. We stayed there five years.

Zenon   Jan   Regina

Panchgani Sanatorium

13 PANCHGANI, INDIA

Funded in part by gold which they had smuggled out of Poland in 1939 the Polish government-in-exile established a welfare organization for Polish war refugees giving the highest priority to the welfare and education of Polish children.

They were assisted by the American Red Cross and British authorities.

Transports out of Iran were arranged to take the refugees to Mexico, India and British Colonies in the East and South Africa regions as well as New Zealand. This began within weeks of the first Polish refugees arrival in Iran. Often they went by boats in convoy during the most treacherous war time shipping.

A select group of women and children arrived in India after traveling over land through Iran. Because of a letter Regina's father had written to the Commandant of the camp they were staying in, Regina and her sister Irene and the two younger boys were allowed to stay together in India.

There was a Polish children's camp in Balachodi near Jarmnagar on the Kathiawan Peninsula. It held six hundred children between the ages of three and fifteen, most were orphans but some had fathers in the Polish Army.

There was plenty of food but the children were found taking bread and fruit to bed with them hiding it under their pillows. They were still in poor physical health and severe demoralization.

I was thirteen when we came to India in 1943. We went to a school taught by Polish teachers. We don't know, we thought Poland would be independent and we would go back.

In India we had barracks with mats on the floor. Three meals a day, it was better. The Polish government-in-exile was supporting us and they bought food and we had three rupees per month. In summer time we usually had some knitting or crochet or reading but we were strictly in orphanage. You get up at 7:30, have to wash or whatever, ate breakfast at 8:00 usually coffee, slices of bread and butter and jam then go to school. 12:00 o'clock was dinner, then siesta for two hours, it was hot, really was time to be inside. Then supper about 5:00 or 6:00, then you have some free time, not much to do so at 9:00 had to be in bed.

In that camp were five thousand people, it was a transit camp, a quarter of a million people went through it; in Africa there were bigger camps and orphanages.

Later, we slept on a bed made with rope binding twine, stretched between poles. We had an oven, don't have no wood so we burned cotton dried stalks and when the oven was hot you throw dough in and it grow, you just scoop it and pick it up.

When I came out of labor camps I was just skin and bones.

I was sent to sanatorium because I was still having fevers. They sent me from Bombay to Khalapur. We were supposed to go to Africa but my father wrote a letter 'Don't separate the children' he said.

We lived in a big camp, five thousand people. I was sent to Sanitarium it was in Poona up in the mountains. Stayed for almost two years, my brothers went with me. The orphanage rented a villa, thirty five kids all together. There were different buildings for TB patients. My sister stayed in Khalapur and my father was still in the army.

My brothers went to school, a Polish school, sickly kids only went a couple of hours a day. Short lessons so we wouldn't get too tired. I was in sanatorium from 1942 to 1945, in and out. I would go back to barracks for a while then back in again.

In 1944 I made confirmation in Panchgani at the Catholic Church, the Bishop was there. Small church, a deaf old priest heard our confessions. We didn't know a word of English and he didn't know Polish. He had a big tube he held up to his ear.

We had a card with ten main sins listed on it, at the bottom was the Hail Mary and the Our Father. He had one in English I had in Polish. I would point to one and he would look at his card, when done he pointed to one of the prayers at the bottom. He held up his fingers to say how many times to say them. At Confirmation we had one couple for everybody, she was for the girls and the man was for the boys.

Jan   Zenon   Regina   Irene

India 1944

Just south of Bombay lies Panchgani, which means 'five hills' in Hindu. It was a resort located inland from the city of Poona. On the top of one of these hills was a large sanatorium which at that time was treating one thousand four hundred tuberculosis patients. Regina had finally been diagnosed as having Pleurisy which is also a disease of the lungs. It causes the patient to have recurrent bloody coughing spells; making it very painful to breathe. Fevers would come and go leaving her debilitated, unable to get well.

There was also a Polish refugee camp in Valivade, Kolhapur, just South of Panchgani, which was home to 5,000 Polish refugees.

There were rows and rows of buildings made with bamboo and mats, one hundred fifty plus barracks, Mess halls, communal baths, a school and a church made up the compound. Each barrack held fifty beds to a side with a room for a guardian. They were made with bamboo, red tile roofs and dirt floors. No windows only openings which you could slide shut during the night so the snakes and monkeys couldn't get in.

Regina, her two brothers, and sister were taken to the temporary village. When she wasn't in the hospital Regina would join them in the camp.

The civilians, that is families or children with a parent, stayed in other barracks. They got money from the Polish government to buy groceries. They had charcoal grills to cook on.

Besides school, lessons were given in typing, knitting and how to crochet. Adults would farm the available land, dances were held as well as church celebrations.

The food was good, eggs, butter and milk along with curries, fruits and vegetables. For both the TB patients and for Regina treatment was the same, rest, good food and sun.

Both in the camp and the sanatorium the children dressed in uniforms. The girls wore gray skirts and white blouses and the boys gray shirts and shorts, both wore roman sandals.

When she was finally discharged from the hospital Regina convalesced in one of the Polish villas at Panchgani before returning to the Valivedi Refugees camp. Regina's father sent money to his children, they had some woman sew dresses for them. They also got clothes from the USA through UNICEF.

World War II ended May 7, 1945 in the European theater when the Germans surrendered. But the refugees stayed at the camp and in most of the camps around the world where they had been sent.

When India won her independence on August 15, 1947, they decided it was time for the refugees to go back home, back to Poland.

At the beginning of the war they had agreed to host 10,000 refugees which included 5,000 orphans. But they, as did the other countries harboring the Poles felt it was time for them to return to their own country.

The Polish Red Cross had been instrumental in placing the children in the camps and now they would be involved in sending them home.

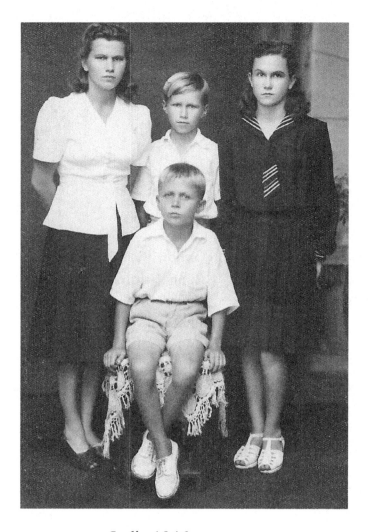

India 1946

Irene   Zenon   Regina
Jan

14 STEFAN

From the very beginning when they were forced to leave their home in Poland, Stefan Siminski tried to keep his family together.

He struggled in the slave labor camp in Siberia and when Hitler invaded the Soviet Union he agreed to join the Polish Army being formed by the Allies.

Under this guise he and his children left Russia and fled to other Soviet controlled provinces. Unable to travel, his wife had to be left behind in a hospital.

Knowing that orders for release could be revoked at any time, they fled for their lives along with exiles from all over Russia, Siberia, Vorkuta and the Ural mountains.

Hard labor camps, prisons, forests and mines, wherever Stalin had slaves were emptying, people dragging themselves toward Persia.

When he could he kept his children with him, through the long ride out of Siberia to the kolkhoz' of Uzbekistan. When the work ran out, no longer able to feed and shelter them, he placed the younger ones in an orphanage. Irene was sent to join the youth corps and he and his oldest son, Edmund, joined the Polish army.

While in the army Stefan contracted malaria and became severely ill. He was mustered out. Once again he found the children and took them with him.

He always kept in touch, writing letters. He wrote the commandant of the camp where the children were staying, asking him to find a Doctor who could find out why Regina was so sick, why she kept getting fevers.

He wrote the International Red Cross in 1943 to locate his oldest daughter Cecylia. She had not been at home in Rejmontwicze when the Russians had forced them from their farm. She was away at school and as a result was left in Poland. They forwarded his letter to her. She was alive, still in Poland, however, it would be many years before he would see her again.

Over a period of five years Regina was treated, in and out of the hospital. During this time his children, Irene, Regina, Zenon and Jan stayed in India waiting for the end of the war.

His wife, Ann, unable to recover from malnutrition and debilitation, died in Tehran. She is buried in a small Catholic cemetery there. Hundreds of tombstones are inscribed with the same year, 1942. Almost two thousand Polish men, women and children are buried there far from their homes and loved ones.

Despite his age, Stefan was once again recalled to the army. This time he would be sent to Palestine where he joined Ander's Army and began to train for the battles in Italy.

The following letters written to Stefan were translated by Zofia Klaczak Rombach, Grayling Michigan

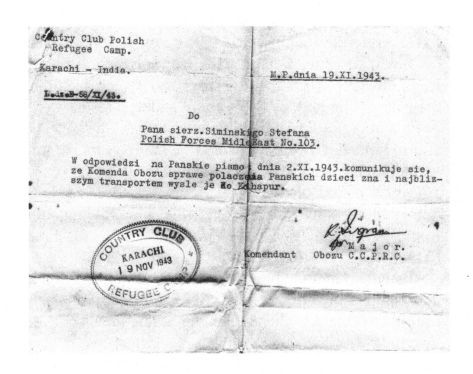

Country Club Polish
Refugee Camp.

Karachi - India.   M.P. dnia Nov. 19. 1943

To Mr. Stefan Siminski
Polish Forces MidleEast No. 103.

In response to the letter of 11/12/43 communications with your kids have been made. The kids will soon be transferred to the compound.

Major Commander Obozu.
Country Club

Cynthia Clark

```
Starostwo Osiedla Polskiego
Valivade, k/Kolhapur.                    Valivade, dnia 29.grudnia 1943
L.dz. 560/II/43
                    Naczelny Lekarz
                    Szpitala Osiedla Valivade

        Proszę o jaknajrychlejsze podanie mi stanu zdrowia
Reginy Siminskiej, pozostajacej w szpitalu Laxmi.
        Proszę o wyczerpująca diagnozę, gdyż muszę tele-
graficznie zawiadomić o tym ojca.
        Równocześnie proszę podać jakie dziecko ma samopo-
czucie.
        Sprawa bardzo pilna.
                                        Starosta Osiedla :
                                        (W. Jagiellowicz)
```

front

Starostwo, Osiedla Polskiege
Valivade, Kolhapur   Dec. 29. 1943

        Kolhapur Clinic
        To the director of this clinic,

Please let me know about the conditions of Regina Siminski.

She was hospitalized in the Laxmi hospital.

I want to know all of the diagnostics, and how she is feeling; so that I can tell her father.

It is very important.

.   clinic
                              (W. Jagiettowicz)

back

The estate vailvade

After consolation with our doctor about Regina Siminski, she is doing well. The diagnosis is pneumonia.

Valivade 1.1.44

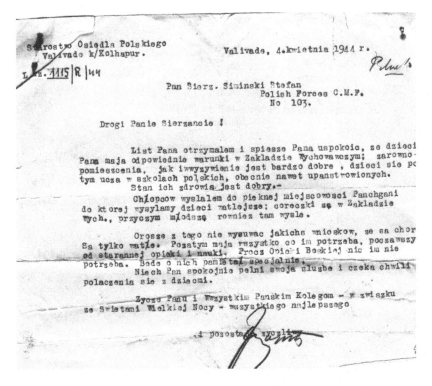

Kolhapur Clinic 4 April 1944
Valivade k/Kolhapur.

> To Mr. Stefan Siminski,
> Polish Forces C.M.F.
> No. 103.

Dear Mr. Siminski:

I received a letter from you, and I will respond that your kids are in the clinic, and are attending school. They are doing well. The boys are studying Panchgan, and the daughters are going to the same place too.

The kids are not real sick, just weak. They have everything that they need. They just need care and be loved, that's all. I wish you serve your country in peace and do not worry about your kids; you will be reunited with them. I wish every service man good luck and happy holidays.

Pozosta Zyczliwy

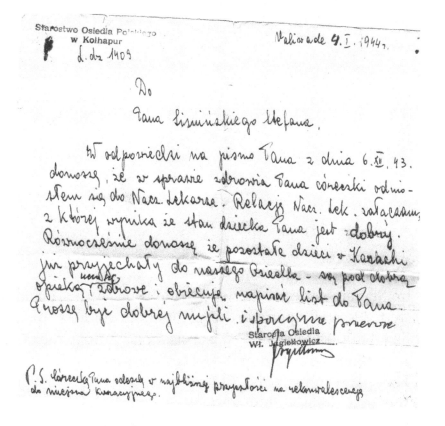

Starostwo Osiedia Polekiego   Valivade 4.11.1944
w Kolhapur

To Mr. Stefan Siminski,
In response to the test of 6/12/43, the report on the health of your daughter was made by the chief of physician. The doctor said that your child's condition is good. I aslo want to tell you that your kids were transferred to our clinic. They got very good care and they will write you a letter soon, and please be in good spirits and think positive that everything will be ok.
                       Starosta Osiedla
                       Wl. Jagielkowicz

P.S. Your daughter and kids are ok.

15 ANDERS ARMY

In September of 1939 when the Red Army invaded Eastern Poland approximately 200,000 soldiers of the Polish Army had been taken as prisoners. Among them the officers who were slain in the Katyn massacre.

They were transferred first to a prisoner of war camp then exiled along with thousands of Polish civilians to the extreme cold of Siberia. To the forced labor camps.

In 1941 when Stalin broke with Hitler he agreed to establish a 'Polish Regiment' within the Red Army. They would use the prisoners that had survived and take in volunteers. General Wladyslaw Anders was released from the Lubanyka prison and put in charge of the men. They numbered seventy thousand including thousands of exiled Polish civilians. His regiment would become known as Anders Army.

Training camps were set up in Soviet held provinces in Uzbekistan and Kazakhstan. General Anders convinced the Russians that the men needed time to recover and train. Supplies including food and uniforms would be paid for by the Allies.

After the Katyn massacre was exposed and Stalin once more closed the gates of the labor camps, 'Anders Army' left the Soviet Union to join the British High Command in the Middle East. They had training camps in Palestine and one of their most historic battles was the battle of Monte Cassino in May 1944.

At the age of fifty, Stefan went to Palestine for basic training. The army knew about his farming background so they put him in charge of a mule brigade.

They soon had orders to proceed to Italy where they would help the Allies battle Germans in the mountains. First they must take the town of Monte Cassino.

Monte Cassino is in the Italian Aurunci Mountains which were thought to be impassable. There is a hilltop Abbey situated at the height of the mountain, it became the linchpin of the battle. The area was heavily fortified with mountain defenses and difficult river crossings. The task of capturing Monastery Hill was given to the Poles.

The Polish Infantry was placed in the mountains and on the ridges and valleys north of Cassino. Stefan and the other men in charge of the mules led them across seven miles of goat tracks and rocky terrain. The mules were tethered to each other with rope, thirty to a train. Loaded with ammunition and supplies they were exposed to accurate military fire from the Germans entrenched on the top of the mountain. The soldiers in charge of the mule trains soon named the area 'Death Valley'.

In the end the Germans were finally defeated which opened the road north to Rome. The Poles had faced three of the Germans best divisions and had pushed them back. In doing so, they suffered more than 11,000 casualties.

When the Germans surrendered in 1945 General Anders troops stayed in Italy and were engaged in occupation duties. Their presence drew many displaced Poles and released Polish prisoners-of-war to their camps.

When the Teheran-Yalta accords were signed giving Poland to the Soviet Union they were bitterly opposed, they refused to go back to Poland under communist rule, to be ground into submission under Stalin's heel.

In late 1946 after they were stripped of Polish citizenship by the government in Warsaw, the soldiers were transported to the United Kingdom where they were demobilized. Stefan found himself on his way to England, a man without a country.

16 YALTA CONFERENCE

February 4 through 11, 1945, the heads of three governments, the United States, the United Kingdom, and the Soviet Union, met near Yalta in the Crimea at the Livadia Palace.

President Franklin D. Roosevelt, Prime Minister Winston Churchill and Josef Stalin discussed the re-establishment of the nations of war torn Europe along with an agenda for governing post war Germany. The Polish government-in-exile had not been invited to attend.

At the time of the conference the Russian Red Army occupied and held much of Eastern Europe with a military three times greater than the area held by Allied forces in the West.

Churchill believed Stalin to be a 'devil-like tyrant leading a vile system'.

FDR thought by giving Stalin whatever he wanted and not asking for anything in return would make him (Stalin) work for a world of democracy and peace.

Stalin's position was that he felt so strong he could dictate the terms of the conference.

Poland was the first item on the Soviet agenda. Stalin led everyone present to believe he wanted a strong, free and independent Poland. He stipulated that the demands made by the Polish government-in-exile were not negotiable. They had not been invited and would have no say in its outcome.

Eastern Polish territory that had been annexed by Russia in 1939, at the start of the war, was already occupied by the Red Army.

At the time of the conference, 200,000 soldiers of the Polish Armed Forces were serving under the high command of the British Army. Many of them came from the Kresy region of Eastern Poland.

In 1939 they had been sent to the Gulags in Siberia while Russia took over their territory and homes. In 1941 when Churchill and Stalin formed an alliance against Germany the Kresy Poles were released from the slave labor camps to form a regiment called 'Anders Army.'

These troops helped defeat the Germans in North Africa and Italy. They hoped to return to their homes in Kresy in an independent and democratic Poland after the war.

But at the Yalta conference Roosevelt and Churchill largely conceded to Stalin's demands to annex the territory, including Kresy and to carry out Polish population transfers. They had, in fact, agreed that tens of thousands of veteran Polish troops under British command should lose their homes to the Soviet Union with the implication that relatives, including wives and children, would be at the mercy of the NKVD.

In reaction to this news, thirty officers and men from the Corps (Polish regiment) committed suicide.

Churchill defended his actions at Yalta in a debate with Parliament on February 27, 1945 which ended in a vote of confidence. However, many MPs (Members of Parliament) openly criticized him and voiced loyalty to Britain's Polish allies.

When the Second World War ended in May of 1945, a Communist government was installed in Poland. Many Polish soldiers refused to return to Poland. The result of their refusal was the Polish Resettlement Act 1947, Britain's first mass immigration law.

The Western Powers soon realized that Stalin would not honor the free elections in Poland. Churchill wrote Roosevelt about the wholesale deportations and liquidations of opposing Polish citizens by the Soviets.

FDR maintained his confidence in Stalin; he felt that Stalin's early priesthood training had 'entered into his nature of the way in which a Christian gentleman should behave.'

On March 1, Roosevelt assured Congress that he had returned from the Crimea with a firm belief that 'We have made a start on the road to a world of peace.' By March 21, the Ambassador to the US, Averill Harriman, cabled Roosevelt that 'We must come clearly to realize that the Soviet program is the establishment of totalitarianism ending personal liberty and democracy as we know it.'

Two days Later, Roosevelt admitted his view of Stalin had been excessively optimistic and that Averill was right.

Poland was now under complete control of the Soviets.

17 JOURNEY TO ENGLAND

I was in and out of the hospital at the sanatorium. I would go back to the barracks in Valivade and attend school. Largest camp, five thousand women and children. On September 15, 1945 was reunited with my brothers and sister. We stayed there till 1947.

India was getting their independence, didn't want us there, they wanted all refugees out. We knew Churchill and Roosevelt had sold Poland to Russia, we couldn't go back.

All the countries that had accepted Polish refugees wanted them out. India didn't want us any more, took all Polish refugees to England from Mexico, New Zealand and Africa. First took all the army to England.

We were disgusted, the government sent representatives to all the camps. They had lists. They got people to sign to go back to Poland.

Unless you had a job or something, maybe married someone you could stay. They knew if they went back the trains didn't even stop in Poland, went back to Siberia.

Father was already in England, we knew we were going to join him there. Edmund was in army artillery, anti air craft, he was sent to England but don't know where, he find a job somewhere.

We left India September 7, 1947, we were displaced persons, people without a country.

Went on a troop ship, it was luxury. Table cloths and cloth napkins.

SS Empire Brent

The SS Empire Brent began life as the ocean liner the SS Letitia. Requisitioned at the start of WW II she served as an armed merchant cruiser then as a troop ship. Badly damaged in 1943 she was repaired in Canada and became a hospital ship.

Returned to civilian service in 1946 after the end of the war, she was sold and once more renamed, the SS Empire Brent. She sailed between India and the Far East before running an emigration service between the United Kingdom and Australia.

On September 7, 1947 she left Bombay, India and sailed to Southampton with 968 Polish displaced persons aboard.

Among them were Regina, age seventeen listed as a student, Irena, age twenty, Zenon age twelve, student and Jan age ten, student. They arrived in Southampton, England on September 21, 1947 after a voyage of almost a month.

India had taken 10,000 refugees under their care. Mexico allowed 1,432 to be relocated in their country. New Zealand limited the number of orphans to 733 but also took in 105 teachers, Doctors, one priest and a number of administrative officers.

The near East, Iran, British Palestine took 22,000 and Africa welcomed 13,000.

In 1943 the United States secretly took in 706 which included 166 children. Two days later they were shipped to Mexico. That fall a second group of 726 arrived, including 408 children, they were also sent to Mexico.

After the end of the war rather than return to communist Poland many Poles moved to Great Britain, Canada, Australia, Argentina and the USA.

As a result of Soviet conduct in taking over Poland and the consequent repression of Polish citizens the Polish Resettlement Act of 1947 was passed and became Britain's first mass immigration law.

Polish forces formed the fourth largest armed force in Europe during WWII fighting with the British during the Battle of Britain. They were instrumental in the Battle of Monte Cassino, Falaise Gap, Battle of Arnhem and the Siege of Tobruk. The Poles broke the early version of the Enigma code and gave the information to the British.

Churchill in a speech to Parliament said, 'His Majesty's Government will never forget the debt they owe to the Polish troops... I earnestly hope it will be possible for them to have citizenship and freedom of the British empire, if they so desire.'

When Joseph Stalin reneged on his Yalta promise and a Communist government was installed in Poland, thousands of Polish soldiers and their families resettled in England.

At the same time Britain's social and economic areas had been hard hit, to rebuild physically and financially it required a workforce.

The Polish Resettlement Act enabled Poles to settle in Britain and provide needed labor.

18 REUNION

In England my father was discharged as soon as war ended. Older brother, Edmund, was in the army.

My sister Irene, my brothers Zenon and Jan, and I arrived in Southampton, no one met us, they took us to Suffolk for one month quarantined. Come from hot climate, don't know we have disease or something. Took Zenon to hospital. He had a wound on his foot from going barefoot in India. He scratched his ankle, it was swollen, had bugs under the skin. Took him to operate on his leg.

Stayed in Crewe, northwest of Chester, saw my father when I got there. He was not married then. The woman he met in Ahwaz had gone to Africa with her sons. She wrote him asking him to take her to England. Her husband was dead and his brother also wrote him asking him to help her so she would not have to go back to Poland. They got married in 1949.

Stayed in a Norwich compound, Camp C, there was a chemical factory or something like that where my father got a job.

Camps were all Polish, we didn't have interaction with English. I was self taught, we had English as second language in school but only ABC's so forth.

I was busy taking care of my two brothers so they didn't send me to school. Kept an eye on them and worked in mess hall as a waitress. There was an English commandant, a Major with lots of secretaries; they always come in to eat. Worked three hours for breakfast, three hours for lunch and three hours for supper. Set tables, they either ate there or bring containers to take food home. Served them and washed dishes, got paid, a little. Boys were in school. My father found a Scottish woman who gave lessons in English, I went to her.

England 1947
Irene Stefan Jan Edmund Regina
1st reunion. Zenon was in the hospital.

Diddington, Cheshire, England

During WW II the American Army had built a hospital on the grounds of Diddington Park on the Thornhill family estate. One of many English estates, it was transformed first into an Army base, then as a Camp for the relocated Polish refugees. When the Americans left the area in 1945 the hospital was renamed as the Polish Hospital #6 which housed a large maternity unit.

There were large corrugated Nissen and timber framed huts which lined the compound. With communal wash houses, toilet blocks and mess halls, it was a typical army camp still surrounded by barbed wire and watch towers.

The first refugees that were transported to the camp by army trucks were alarmed at the sight. They said it reminded them of a concentration camp, so the wire and towers were quickly removed.

Families were assigned spaces in the huts, their living areas separated by curtains. Children without parents lived in separate units.

As did all the camps, this one held people from all walks of life and every profession. Farmers, teachers, doctors and former soldiers rubbed shoulders with store clerks, writers and cobblers. It was a Polish community, albeit, in a used army base, that allowed life to go on. It gave some stability to people who had been shunted cruelly from pillar to post for years.

A church was established in one of the barracks, Sunday services were well attended.

Schools were formed with Polish teachers, Regina was still looking after her two younger brothers so she didn't attend, instead she found work at the mess hall while they were in school.

There were factories, a cement plant and electrical power plant in the vicinity and some of the men found work outside the camp.

England had lost a lot of her work force and there was much to do, reconstruction of bombed buildings and houses. Food was still scarce and some rationing still going on but all in all it was a safe and stable time.

From this and other camps the Polish people would resume their lives, many choosing to immigrate to the US, Australia and New Zealand. Some chose to stay, many married English subjects.

Eventually the camp emptied and resumed its life as a country estate.

19 ZDZISLAW NIEMCZYCKI

Irene had a girlfriend, Leona, who started writing for unknown soldiers. Leona met Carl and when they got married invited Irene to be her bridesmaid. Irene met her husband George there; when they got married I was Maid of Honor for her.

Their best man was Zdzislaw (John) Niemczycki. I was only seventeen, boys was not on my agenda because I had two brothers to take care of.

John was from the village of Sarny, about two hundred meters from our village. His father was the chief bookkeeper for the Forest Department, his mother was a teacher. When the Russians came John was fifteen years old. Was taken with his mother and other children from his home in Poland sent to Gorki, south of the Archangel triga. His father and oldest brother went into hiding, they stayed in Poland and ran a saw mill close to Warsaw.

I don't know if his father was in the underground but a lot of people who stayed were so it's possible.

Polish Home Army
Armia Krakow (AK)

John Niemczycki' father worked for the forest service in Poland. Unable to stop the Russians from taking his family, he put on his work uniform and with his oldest son, left the area. They stayed in Poland during the war and managed to evade both the Russians and the Germans.

On November 19, 1939, after Hitler and Stalin invaded Poland, two soldiers of the defeated Polish army, Wifold Pilacki and Jan Wlodarkiewicz founded the Secret Polish Army. They started with 8,000 men, both military and civilian, twenty machine guns, and several anti tank rifles.

The Armia Krakow (AK) carried out thousands of armed raids and intelligence operations. They sabotaged hundreds of railway transports and provided the Western Allies with information on the German Concentration Camps, the VI flying bomb and the V2 rocket.

The city of Czortkow was in the western part of what is now the Ukraine. In 1939 it was part of the second Polish Republic and had 19,000 inhabitants, half of whom were Roman Catholic. The 36th Reserve Infantry Division, an important garrison for the Polish Defense Corps, was housed in the city.

The Soviet Union invaded and annexed it in 1939 imprisoning the captured soldiers in the barracks/prison.

On the night of January 21, 1940 the first Polish uprising began in this city. Anti-Soviet Poles, most of them teenagers from the local high schools, their teacher, and a few adults, planned to storm the local Red Army prison and liberate the captured Polish soldiers.

Over one hundred people gathered in the Roman Catholic Church, most of them unarmed, a few had guns or knives, even some had old fashioned swords. They divided themselves into four groups. The first group would seize the main barracks, the second the prison, the third the center of town, and the fourth the rail station.

Their battle cry was 'Z Kyzyem' (With the Cross). At 2200 hours they began the attack on the barracks. Alarmed by gunshots, Soviet troops counter attacked. After a very short fire fight three Soviet soldiers and fourteen Poles lay dead, several more wounded, and the plotters were dispersed.

The next day retaliation was brutal. The NKVD made mass arrests and jailed 150 people. They were interrogated with beatings and kicked until their jaws and ribs were broken. Then twenty four were shot and fifty five were sent to Siberia. What happened to the rest is unrecorded.

This first attempt, by untrained, without experienced leadership, was unsuccessful, but the Poles were even more determined to defend their country against these invaders.

There were nine concentration camps established by the Germans in Poland. The 'undesirables' were interned there, including priests, nuns, gypsies, Catholics, political prisoners and hundreds of thousands of Jews. Little news was getting out to the Western Allies about the camps.

Unable to believe the size and scope of this inhumanity to man many in the outside world refused to believe anything so atrocious was going on.

In 1940 Witold Pilecki, one of the founders of the Polish Home Army, with false identity cards deliberately allowed himself to be caught by the Germans. They sent him along with the other prisoners to the Auschwitz concentration camp. While there, Witold organized the underground operation, 'ZOW' (Zwiazek Organizacji Wojskowej). That October, ZOW sent its first report about the camp and it's genocide program to the Home Army in Warsaw. These reports became the principle source of intelligence on Auschwitz - Birkenaw camps for the Western Allies.

The AK became the most notable resistance in Poland, it absorbed most other underground forces and remained loyal to the Polish government-in-exile. Over time it numbered between 200,000 and 600,000 volunteers and was one of the three largest resistance groups during the European theater in WW II.

By 1942 the Home Army (AK) had turned into a regular division with sixteen infantry, three cavalry, and one motorized brigade. All were equipped with captured weapons.

A Polish youth resistance organization, 'Wawer' from the Wower district of Warsaw, was responsible for minor sabotage operations. Their first action was a series of graffiti in Warsaw commemorating the Warsaw Ghetto Massacre. They painted 'pomscimy Wawer' (We'll avenge Wawer) on Warsaw walls. At first they painted the whole text, then shortened it to two letters, 'P' and 'W'. Not long after, they invented the Kotwica (Anchor) which became the symbol of all Polish resistance in occupied Poland. It was known as the 'sign of the underground Polish Army.'

One of the most daring escapes by Polish prisoners from a concentration camp occurred on June 20, 1942. Three men dressed as members of the SS, fully armed and in an SS staff car, escaped from the Auscwitz concentration camp. They drove out the main gate in a stolen Rudolf Hoss automobile, Steyr 220, with a smuggled report from Witold Pilecki about the Holocaust. They were never caught.

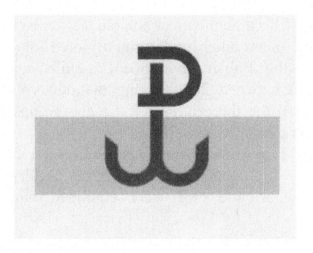

Kotwica (Anchor)

20 RELEASE FROM SIBERIA

Zdzislaw (John) worked in the forest in the Siberian camps in 1941 and he and his family got out when Stalin let the people go. He was almost seventeen and had malaria, dysentery and typhoid. They left the camp and made their way to Uzbekistan.

Now in Uzbekistan when people died they threw them on a pile, dumped lime over the bodies and buried them in a communal grave. John was so sick they thought he was dead, his body was thrown on top of a pile.

When John was a young boy he had a small pox vaccination. He scratched it and then his head; no hair grew on the spots (where he scratched) on his head. A neighbor from his village was walking by the pile of bodies, she recognized the bald spots on his head. She remembered him, walked over to get better look, saw his chest rise a little bit. He was still breathing. They took him to hospital and cured him.

His mother was sent to Nazareth where she taught religion to the girls, his sister and youngest brother, the one with epilepsy, were sent to Victoria Lake in Uganda, Africa. The older brother, one year older than John, went to join the army, Anders Army. He later fought in Bologna and is buried in the Monte Cassino cemetery.

In 1941 Stalin gave the prisoners amnesty and their exodus began from Siberia to Uzbekistan. It was during this evacuation that John, age sixteen wasted by disease, was thought to be dead.

While Regina went to India and then to the sanatorium, John now recovered tried to join Anders Army. Since he was under eighteen he was enlisted in the Youth Corps instead. On his next birthday he was drafted into the Army.

Meanwhile, on the war front, the Germans were advancing on Stalingrad, Russia. By this time the Russians had broken with Hitler and joined the Western allies. The massacre in the Katyn forest had been uncovered, and Stalin shut the door on any more of the prisoners in his labor camps leaving.

On April 19, 1943 the ghetto in Warsaw erupted and the Polish people began to fight back.

21 WARSAW UPRISING

After the Ghetto was obliterated by the Germans, their army took over the city. They had burned and destroyed the homes and businesses in the area where the Jews had been confined. The civilians that weren't killed during the uprising were shipped off to the concentration camps, or executed on site.

On August 1, 1944 while the Russians sat on the outskirts of Warsaw the AK made its move to liberate the city from the Germans. This major operation was to be coordinated with the Red Army approach to the Eastern suburbs. But the Soviets stopped short of their goal purposely allowing the Germans to regroup and eventually demolish the city.

Polish resistance forces fought for sixty three days with little outside help. Churchill pleaded with Stalin but he refused to give any aide to the liberators. He also refused to allow Allied planes to land and refuel on Polish airfields that were under Soviet control.

Even without clearance from the Russians, Churchill sent low level supply drops to the Polish AK, a total of two hundred drops by the Royal Air Force, the South African Air Force and the Polish Air Force.

It is estimated that 16,500 Polish and allied resistance forces died during the uprising. Over 6,000 were badly wounded and from 150,000 to 200,000 Polish civilians were also killed.

Two days after the fighting started, SS General Bach-Zelewski was placed in command of all the German forces in Warsaw. German units came from everywhere, mostly from the infamous Waffen SS penal unit. They were described as a rabble of cut throats, renegades, sadistic and undisciplined rejects from other units.

General Bach-Zelewski's strategy was to go house to house shooting all the inhabitants. On the first day, more than 10,000 civilians, most of them women and children, were killed.

Rape, murder, torture, and fire followed the brigades through the suburbs killing another 30,000 civilians in three days. They entered, killed, then set fire to any hospital in their path, often with patients still inside the buildings.

When the Polish resistance captured two Panther tanks, the Nazis forced civilian women onto their own armored vehicles as human shields. Thousands of Polish people were taken to the railroad yards and executed by mass shootings by the Germans.

After sixty three days, the city was reduced to rubble; the AK was finished. Over 150,000 civilians were killed, 90,000 Polish citizens were sent to labor camps, while 60,000 more were shipped to death camps of Ravensbruck, Auschwitz, Mauthausen and others.

The captured AK's were treated as POWs which outraged Stalin who wanted them killed.

The uprising allowed Germans to destroy the AK as a force, and the main beneficiary turned out to be Stalin. He was able to impose a communist government on post war Poland without fear of armed resistance.

Three months after Warsaw was razed to the ground, the Russian Red Army moved into the city.

22 WARS END

When the war ended, John's mother and the other children went back to Poland. His father was still in Poland and wanted them all to come back home. His mother wanted John to join her.

He was on a train going to meet her when he changed his mind, he got out, didn't go back with them.

I was in Diddington working in kitchen taking care of the boys, my father came on weekends to see us. Father got married in Diddington, brought his wife with her three boys. They all moved to Norwich. Jan and Zenon and I went with them.

In two years John wrote me a Christmas card, he came over for Easter and that's how we started.

We got married in September 2, 1950, my husband he go work in electric power plant in Ipswich. He did anything. We moved into a rented room with kitchen and shared a bathroom with the landlady, rooms were scarce then. Lived there about a year then moved to sister Irene's. She had bought a house in Manchester.

I worked in a sewing factory sewing pajamas, got pregnant, was very sick so quit.

Regina   John
(back) Teresa, stepmother, Stefan

23 IMMIGRATION TO UNITED STATES

Because my father was in USA from 1913 to 1918 he said 'We're going to America.' My father knew Detroit, had been there, had some cousins they sponsored us. You still had to have a sponsor. After the war lots of them couldn't get a sponsor so some churches sponsored them.

Whole family came, not together, older brother came first.

My husband and I had to wait because I was pregnant and the commandant said 'You have no insurance what would you do, stay and have the baby.' So we did. Had Edward in Manchester at St. Mary's hospital.

The Liverpool consulate told us, not supposed to go on welfare for two years (when we got to US). If don't get a job or something, we would be sent back, no place to go. Had to have a sponsor.

My father's cousin lived in Detroit, he had been born in the States but when he was three his family came back to Poland. When the war was on and the United States brought all their people out of Poland, they came back to Detroit. So he was going to sponsor us.

We sailed on the Mauritania to New York, October 1951. With son, four months old, we came to America. Ellis Island was closed, we took a train to Detroit.

Father immigrated in February of 1952 with his wife and sons. My older brother Edmund had already come to the States before any of us.

Cecylia stayed in Poland, in 1962 she went to the Embassy in Warsaw, wanted a visiting visa, just to see us. The ambassador said 'No I'm not going to give you a visitor's visa, ask your father to send you papers. You are going to stay there, you won't care, you're going to stay.' So he would do it, give a permit, do it officially.

So she wrote a letter and sent the papers and she came in 1962.

Zenon and Jan came to live with my husband and me, then Edmund came. Irene and her husband moved to Windsor, Canada. It was just across the river from Detroit so still close to family.

Each country was better and better, India was poor country but better, we 'got out of hell'. We had a mess hall, three meals a day. England was even better. In the United States we went to father's cousin, his house was so big. All the houses were so big, lots of rooms inside. Living room, dining room, kitchen, bedrooms, outside large yards.

One thing I didn't like was all the gray porches. I thought they should be red. Don't know why, even in England they were gray, but thought they should all be red.

We came on Friday, November 1, 1951. On Monday John get his social security card, and started work on Thursday. He painted and fixed cars for a Chevy dealer, he was never without work.

Had very little English but it was heaven on earth.

Regina   John

EPILOGUE

Regina, John and their son, Edward, arrived in Detroit on November 1, 1951. They settled there for the next twenty eight years. Adding another son, Chester and a daughter, Maria to their family.

Irene and her husband moved to Windsor, Canada. They found a home just across the river from Detroit. Still close to family.

Edmund lived and worked in Detroit, he married late in life and they lived in St. Clair Shores.

Cecylia came to visit and stayed. She and her family also settled in St. Clair Shores.

Jan married and had four children. He divorced and now lives in New Hudson with one of his sons.

Zenon worked on the space project in California and makes his home there.

Stefan arrived with his wife and the five boys in February of 1952. They lived with Regina and John and Stefan found a job at the new Grace hospital. He made minimum wage.

They later moved into their own house in Detroit and Jan and Zenon went to live with Regina.

When their neighborhood changed Stefan moved to Reed City and bought a small house. He died in 1983. His wife died in 2000.

John   Regina

Regina   Edward   Chester   John

John always dreamed of having a farm, saw an ad in the Detroit Times for sixty acres with ponds in Luther, Michigan. He and my father drove up to look at it, they liked it, only $45 an acre. We had no money and no one would loan us any so we mortgaged our house in Detroit.

Over the next eighteen years came up every weekend and holiday, remodeling that dilapidated house. In 1980 moved from Detroit to the farm. John opened a body shop in one of the barns.

John   Maria   Edward (back)   Chester

He lived only eighteen months after we moved, died at age 56.

Had to make a decision, children were all grown, boys in Detroit, daughter out East. Either sell the farm and move back or sell the house in Detroit and stay. Prayed and prayed about it. Then one Sunday Father gave a sermon and he answered my question. I never told him about my problem but his sermon told me what to do. Holy Spirit spoke through him and I made my decision.

Regina still resides on her farm in Luther, Michigan and attends services at St. Ignatius Catholic Church.

Edward

Chester   Regina   Maria

Zenon and Regina, 2013

References

NKVD Peoples Commissariat for Internal Affairs Http://NKVD.ORG: TheMemorialPage 2-7-2013

History of Samarkand "Ancient Silk Road" www.Advantour.com 2-10-2013

Thaddeus M. Machrowicz www.Poles.org/db/m.names/Machrowicz 1/25/2013

Yalta Conference www.history.State.govmilestones/1937-1945/Yalta 1/25/2013

Wladyslaw Sikorski www.en.Poland.gov.pl/Wladyslaw,Sikorski:,(1881-1 11/2/2012

Kotlas and the Gulag http:/www.kotlas.org/kotlas/history/sybert.htm. 9/22/2012

Monte Cassino Battlefield tour http://nuke.montecassinotour.com/THECONTRIBUTIONOFANDERSARMYATCASSINO/tabid/79/Default.aspx 1/6/2013

The Struggle for Poland http:/www.pbs.org/behindcloseddoors/in-depth/struggle-Poland.htm. 9/19/2012

Compilation from Exiled to Siberia - J. T. Gross, Keith Sword, Anita Pasdua-Kozicka-anonymous-Klaus Hergt http://info-poland.buffalo.edu/KH.html 8/2/2012

Katyn Massacre Memorial
http://www.electronicmuseum.ca/Poland-WW2/katyn-memorial
8/2/2012

Wall/madden-committee/ ½/2013

Exodus Polish Refugees http://www.parstimes.com/history/polish-refugees/exodusRussia.html 11/24/2012

Polish Resettlement Camps in the UK 194-1969
www.polishresettlementcampsintheUK 2/7/2013

National Archives www.legislation.gov.uk/ukpga/Geo6/10-1
2/7/2013

Polish Military www.polishmilitaria.cm/articles-details.p
12/10/2012

Maria VanderLinden An Unforgettable Journey (1992)
www.antovanz.net//BIBILOTEKA/Linden/1 1/26/2013

Polish Resettlement Act www.legislation.gov.uk/ukpga/Geo6/10-11/19 1/25/2013

ABOUT THE AUTHOR

Cynthia grew up in Detroit, Michigan during WWII, her home a beehive of activity hosting service men on leave. As an adult she earned her ADN and worked as an Emergency Room Nurse across the United States. As a volunteer RN for the Red Cross she assisted during Katrina and local disasters; she also assisted in her local Free Clinic for the uninsured.

Cynthia is married to Chester. They have five children and twelve grandchildren, she has managed to follow her passion to travel, see the world and now share stories of the people she has met, who have added to her life in so many ways.

Cynthia is the author of "A Bite of Life" - a collection of short stories from her life and travels.

You may contact her at gaudemaude@gmail.com.

Made in the USA
Las Vegas, NV
05 October 2021